Earn a Million Plus

EARN A MILLION PLUS

THE LITTLE-KNOWN HIGH-INCOME
OCCUPATION OF MEDIA BUYER

BRUCE CRAN

NEW YORK

LONDON • NASHVILLE • MELBOURNE • VANCOUVER

EARN A MILLION PLUS

The Little Known High-Income Occupation of Media Buyer

Published in New York, New York, by Morgan James Publishing. Morgan James is a trademark of Morgan James, LLC. www.MorganJamesPublishing.com

Proud partner with Ingram Publishing

Morgan James BOGO™

A **FREE** ebook edition is available for you or a friend with the purchase of this print book.

CLEARLY SIGN YOUR NAME ABOVE

Instructions to claim your free ebook edition:
1. Visit MorganJamesBOGO.com
2. Sign your name CLEARLY in the space above
3. Complete the form and submit a photo of this entire page
4. You or your friend can download the ebook to your preferred device

ISBN 9781631955792 paperback
ISBN 9781631955808 ebook
Library of Congress Control Number:
2021935219

Cover Design by:
Sang Le

Interior Design by:
Chris Treccani
www.3dogcreative.net

Morgan James
PUBLISHING

Builds

with...
Habitat for Humanity®
Peninsula and
Greater Williamsburg

Morgan James is a proud partner of Habitat for Humanity Peninsula and Greater Williamsburg. Partners in building since 2006.

Get involved today! Visit MorganJamesPublishing.com/giving-back

TABLE OF CONTENTS

LIST OF ILLUSTRATIONS

INTRODUCTION:

THE LITTLE-KNOWN HIGH-INCOME OCCUPATION

My name is Bruce Cran, and I want *you* to earn a million dollars—or more. I want to pay Media Buyers, and some of the best examples are independent affiliates. *This could be you.*

I spent almost a decade at University doing what I believed I had to do to become successful: learning, studying, and working. Earning degrees. This was years ago, and back then the internet barely existed. Knowledge was contained in books and even if those books could have been digitized, the computers available to the average person didn't have enough memory to hold even a short book such as this one. It was basically the Stone Age.

But from my life as a student and my success as a trial lawyer, let's fast-forward to today where I am an accomplished businessman with wealth beyond my young self's wildest dreams. One thing has become crystal clear: *You cannot learn the fast-paced online world in a university.* You can only learn it from hard work and self-study—or in the way a good lawyer is trained, through mentorship.

The things that are real and worth learning aren't available to you in textbooks. Textbooks make money for people who sell textbooks, and that's about it. Sitting in a classroom with two hundred other students is an exercise in wasted time. It is through *experience*, real work with your sleeves rolled up for hours on end that you will come to truly understand the online space and the various ways to make money there, as I have.

The practical understanding of e-commerce is especially essential when it comes to performance marketing. Performance marketing is where the tire meets the pavement with direct-to-consumer sales and holds potential for huge profits—but you don't get paid unless you achieve the desired result.

True performance marketing is only achieved when you can independently measure results with close to 99% accuracy, *and that only exists in online marketing.*

Imagine trying to do a Cost Per Acquisition (CPA) campaign in a print magazine, such as *People*. You place your advertising that asks your potential customers to call or mail a response to buy your product—you even offer them a code to enter that identifies the magazine where they saw the ad. Orders come from the phone, they come in the mail, but what percentage of the sales can you actually attribute to *People* magazine? More importantly, how much does it cost you to do this forensic work? And how long does it take?

I've been there and done it all in the Stone Age of print. The short answer is it takes months of time to find answers and you're lucky if you come out with 50% accuracy. If you're being paid for every customer you created with your ad in the print magazine, do you accept 50 cents on the dollar? No, of course not. Well, you might say just double the CPA, but the result is too imprecise, and the payouts would jump around like an EKG heart-reading in the hospital room of a trauma victim.

The upshot: True performance marketing has never worked in traditional marketing because you cannot efficiently and effectively track the results.

Now imagine instead that you place a banner advertisement on the *People* website. You simply give the advertisement its own URL with a tracking code and *any customer that comes to the product from that URL is automatically tracked.* Moreover, you collect the browser fingerprint of the customer, which creates a unique identifier of their visit, so even if they return from a different URL—*you know who that customer is.* Browser fingerprints work by creating a unique key or label for a device, combining aspects such as IP address, browser version, monitor resolution, and plug-ins used. *People* will receive credit for the sale and certainly credit for the clicks on their website. You get your fair pay-out.

Thus, performance marketing is driven by the ability to track and report in *real time*. You generate sales or leads and accurately and efficiently track the information (plus more) to get actual credit (actual money) for your work. Performance marketing relies on meeting metrics—concrete, measurable targets—to get yourself paid. Platforms such as email, Google AdWords, Facebook and the like, need to be used and developed as they relate to classic direct marketing.

Convincing a consumer on the spot to buy the product or service you're pitching is the true talent of the new, unheralded position of "Media Buyer." And a great Media Buyer is someone I will gladly pay a million dollars a year or more because they generate sales and brand recognition for my company.

You probably have questions... Good. The world is full of people promising outlandish amounts of money for little to no work. But this isn't that, not by a longshot. Buying media is multidisciplinary hard work and an occupation that has not yet achieved mainstream understanding or recognition. There are no movies, TV shows, novels, or songs available about affiliates and Media Buyers, but if cash rules the world, there will be soon.

Who is a Media Buyer? An affiliate? What do they do? What are they like? How do you become one? How do you know if you have the skills to *succeed* as a Media Buyer? Why would I, Bruce Cran, pay you a million dollars to buy media for my company—and why not just set up a website and wait for traffic?

These are great questions. In answering them, let me tell you a bit more about myself.

I was born in a small town in Australia and shortly thereafter moved to what was then a small town in Canada, in the 1970s. I was lucky enough to study computer science and business in the 1980s, and I graduated as a lawyer in the early 1990s.

The internet was still in its infancy at that time, but I worked hard to apply modern technologies and techniques to my tradecraft of trial law. I had some early successes and secured many clients: my clients liked the brash young attorney who was willing to represent them in marketing and insurance disagreements around the world. My client locations ranged from New York to Tokyo, and by 1998, I was spending most of my time with marketing companies and consulting on building databases that complied with burgeoning global privacy laws. My firm was also providing more and more services that weren't law related, such as database warehouse construction under Extract Transform and Load (ETL) principles.

With my exposure to the world of e-commerce, I witnessed the rise of a never-before-seen occupation, one both intriguing and perplexing in its global nature and outcome. I saw people who, at first glance, could only be employed at the most menial of jobs, suddenly generating extremely large and meaningful incomes.

From dishwashers to trial lawyers, those who could uniquely understand the swiftly evolving online work of early media buying were making big money, shoulder-to-shoulder. Needless to say, my interest was piqued.

So, I made friends with these people. It was to my advantage to do so, but I also had a curious admiration: What they were doing was unlike anything I had ever seen, and how they were doing it was unlike everything I thought I understood about business. These early Media Buyers, these affiliates I met, were running their businesses from coffee shops, shisha clubs, and vape shops. From all walks of life, the affiliates, or early Media Buyers, shared a number of attributes including a strong intuitive understanding of social media and a real social bond. They would come together at huge global gatherings, at events such as Affiliate World or Affiliate Summit, which attract thousands of attendees.

These affiliates tended to be:

- Young; few if any were over the age of thirty
- Full of a sense of camaraderie
- Shy and yet desirous of being noticed and making their mark on the world, they wanted that mark to be seen
- Smart, but not in the "I just spent a decade in university" way; they possessed a kind of "street smarts"
- Risk-takers, lovers of life
- Great with games and mathematics

- Respectful of rules and the establishment, but willing to do *anything* to get ahead

Affiliates, or, as we very first called them, publishers, were the first Media Buyers working on a paid commission. They were a direct result of the internet—the concept had existed for at least a decade, but it wasn't until widespread acceptance of the internet that Media Buyers gained a voice and true presence.

Networks of traffic evolved and before long a viable marketplace emerged for buying clicks at one price and selling them at another. From this place, the platforms and methods for using skills to buy media and exploit systems of arbitrage began to stand out.

Media Buyers are the people who exploit the price difference of a click from a provider to a buyer. The provider can be email, Google, Facebook—any platform that provides clicks. Clicks are the lifeblood of the Media Buyer. It's tempting to want to call a Media Buyer someone who buys commodities, but that would be incorrect. Buying and selling clicks is only part of their game.

A classic commodity futures buyer tries to predict whether the price of a commodity is going to go up or down—say, for example, pork futures—and they speculate based on that prediction. Yet, taking my example of pork: A futures trader with an ability to say how good a pig is will not make the pork belly more valuable. A Media Buyer, on the other hand, *marries the futures buyer's skills with the skills of a performance marketer.* Media Buyers increase their own value.

So, Media Buyers are much more than just mathematical arbitrage; they need to understand excellent marketing. The game isn't just "buy low, sell high." It's about convincing the media provider to sell low to you, while convincing the client to pay a higher price. *Excellent advertising* is what allows the Media Buyer to convince these parties to do this. And not only to convince them but have them clamoring to do so.

Media buying is an entirely new online occupation, only recently existing, which will continue to grow and grow until Hollywood comes along to make the movie about it. Hopefully that movie can showcase the next Gordon Gecko and become the current *Wall Street*: This coming decade will produce new Media Buyers who are all about greed. Because greed is good. *Greed is very, very good.*

Why would I say this? For most people, greed is thought of as a negative characteristic; and in many contexts, it probably is. But not in this business—*definitely* not in performance marketing.

Performance marketing is on the sharp, brutal edge of capitalism. You either sell your product or you don't, and the results are available in real-time. There are a limited number of dollars in a system, and your product is in direct competition with *all the other products for those dollars.* Every dollar you generate is not just a dollar for you, it is also a dollar someone else didn't get.

In essence, you want more than your "fair share" of the market. That's what capitalism is all about. You want to use your talents and abilities to get *more* than you would be allotted as one out of 7,800,000,000 persons on earth… Much more.

Consider what the Media Buyer is actually doing. To be able to buy a click at one price and sell it at a higher price—to make money doing so—the Media Buyer must *make that click meaningful*. The Media Buyer adds value to the click.

Clicks need to generate sales. The more sales a thousand clicks can generate, the more significant the gap becomes between what the Media Buyer *paid* for those clicks and what they *sold* those clicks for. This very quickly expands to exponential significance.

A great Media Buyer strives to do three key things: pay less for each click; sell each click for more; and generate a higher percentage of sales per click. They want that sharp edge; they want to out-perform and out-earn everyone around them. *They want more.* And when they get more, they want more still. This is what I mean by greed, and it is good.

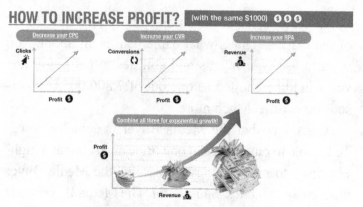

Figure 1. How to increase profit.

Currently, there's a major shortage of people with the particular disposition and skillset of the high-end Media Buyer. Every day the actions of the major platforms increase the demand for excellent Media Buyers. Google sells the best position for search results and as the world transitions to mobile devices, the advertisements become more prominent than ever. We've become accustomed to Google feeding us a few crappy summarized search results, which don't actually take us where we want to go, then accompanying these with up to four advertisements. Facebook, on the other hand, actively restricts access to brand postings in most countries, forcing the brand to pay to reach their followers.

As I write this, I run a performance marketing and advertising agency with hundreds of millions in sales worldwide. My partners and I manage factory workers, we have talented executives, hundreds of excellent staff to ensure great customer service, tech-savvy programmers, creative-minded designers, and hard-working developers. We have people who make the tea and the coffee. There is almost nothing we don't have.

But of the hundreds and hundreds of people who work for us, we have fewer than twenty Media Buyers! Media Buyers are the elite within companies such as mine for important reasons.

First and foremost, the excellent ones are lone wolves. They work by themselves, they don't play in the pack, and they keep their secrets close. They are tightly wound, and most companies actively discourage these sorts of characteristics in their employees. I have a hard time picturing a Media Buyer at a corporate team-building exercise.

Second, the executive world of today does not truly understand *and does not appreciate* what it takes to hire and retain the sort of Media Buyer who can transform a middling company into one that earns hundreds of millions in sales. And if the grass is greener in other pastures, the Media Buyer will seek it out. Ironically, this happens because of what's integral to making Media Buyers so good at what they do.

Third, because most Media Buyers don't have what corporations consider "normal" personalities, they are difficult to fit into existing structures. They are too often placed in circumstances that create needless obstacles to their success, and this frustrates and undermines any great Media Buyer.

Without offending them—or maybe I should offend them, they can take it—on the whole, my great friends who are Media Buyers, are people who are:

- Gamblers when it comes to using other people's money
- Risk-averse in terms of their takeaway from a deal
- Willing to stretch limits
- Likely to remember the best buys and forget the catastrophes
- Stubborn about their beliefs and complicated to convince
- Limited in their respect for those who can't talk about media buying at the level they intuitively understand

These are not easy people, and they're not straightforward to work with. So, with all of these complications, why do we even need Media Buyers?

The answer is simple: With the right assets, Media Buyers bring in customers and make money. Not just one customer for your local pizza restaurant, not a dozen for your favorite retail outlet, *but thousands of customers per hour for any online product or service you can possibly imagine*. That is the revolution that is currently happening, which even the captains of industry do not understand. The multiplicative impact on top-line sales from the addition of paid media cannot be underestimated. The potential is unlimited. And we are at the very beginning.

Do you have what it takes to do this high-paid little-known profession? Am I going to be the one paying you a million dollars a year, or more? Let's talk about it.

Let's find out.

CHAPTER 1:

ARE YOU A MEDIA BUYER?

Before getting into a relationship, it's customary to go on a few dates. You meet, you talk and get to know one another on a first date, and then maybe if it's going well there'll be a second, a third, and even a fourth date before you commit. If you feel strongly enough about each other, you become exclusive.

In this way, I met my co-founder, Jordan Rolband, and DFO Global Performance Commerce, as it's now known, began its journey to becoming the incredible success it is today.

In the early 2010s my business was still handled offline, but I had a keen interest and a need to bring it online. The old model wasn't working anymore. A mutual (and wise) friend connected me with Jordan, who had a diverse skill set and was a senior person at a performance marketing and advertising company called MediaWhiz. The initial set-up was a plan to bring my company in as a client of Jordan's.

Our first date was planned at a conference in Las Vegas in October of 2012. Unfortunately, Jordan had an untimely death in his family and our initial meeting was postponed. We connected a month later in New York City and spent three hours at a Starbucks café. We hit it off immediately.

Our second date was at an affiliate event in Las Vegas in January of 2013. We spent more time together and met with industry people. I was beginning to understand more clearly how the industry worked and functioned and I started to see how Jordan and I might proceed.

Our third and final date was in Vancouver, British Columbia, in February of 2013. Jordan and I left that meeting with the intention of my company coming to MediaWhiz within the month.

But the more Jordan and I talked and exchanged ideas, the more it became clear to both of us that the best fit was to work together and build something unique. We wanted to do much more than we had been doing, and we each recognized that the other had a complimentary skillset. It was one of those rare opportunities that was too good to pass up. The timing was excellent, too: MediaWhiz was in the process of a not-popular acquisition, which opened two doors for Jordan. He could stay at MediaWhiz and be rewarded with raises, stock, and bonuses, or he could try his hand at being an entrepreneur again.

Our plan to build a small, private affiliate network emerged. On August 1, 2013, the first day of live traffic coursed through our network. Direct Focus Online, "DFO" as it was known then, was born.

At this point, the network was our only business. Our focus was on third party nutraceutical offers and one in-house offer. We had no internal media buying teams and worked with only a few hundred affiliate partners. We were ten people in two offices with a shared drive to succeed.

Our company looks very different now.

Our network business is concentrated on e-commerce and comprises twenty internal Media Buyers and more than three thousand affiliate partners who focus on several home-grown products and brands, including some of the most well-known Direct To Consumer (DTC) and Fortune 500 brands, such as, for example, Colgate.

Our brand-building business specializes in sourcing, developing, and marketing superior products and experiences directly to consumers.

Our technology arm develops proprietary Customer Relationship Management (CRM) and Content Management Systems (CMS) technology that makes it easy to create websites, maximize conversions, and connect with global consumers.

We are 350 people across offices on five continents, and we're growing every day. It started with a coffee shop date. You and I can do the same.

Sit down, let's have a chat. Ask me your questions, and I'll ask mine.

Are you a media buyer?

Let Me Buy You a Coffee, Let's Find Out

Can You Produce and Recognize Great Advertising?

Great advertising is the lifeblood of the Media Buyer. Great advertising produces great results and your big pay day. This is the common thread of *Mad Men*, TV, radio, print, and online sales. But with the advent of online marketing, advertising has also become consumable content.

There is one enormous difference between the old days and today: if you can *entertain* the users of Google and Facebook, your traffic is cheaper!

You did not misread that. Would you think that great commercials could ever become *cheaper* than lousy ones? No. Not with a traditional mindset. And yet the fact is that running great ads on Google and Facebook *costs less than running bad ones*. Platforms don't want to run bad ads because their users do not want to see them.

With TV, radio, and print media, people will tend to grin and bear it; they might temporarily flip the channel, they'll turn a page, but generally they'll sit through. Online is a different beast. People leave the site, and the platform loses them. Moreover, *they know they've lost them*. And it all happens so fast. There is too much else out there to see on the web. Customers *expect* to be entertained.

So, the key is *great* advertising, and the platforms are willing to reward you for that by lower costs per click and better placements. Entertaining advertising not only keeps customers on the site but generates thousands of clicks, and ultimately sales.

Produce clicks, and you can media buy. To do this you'll need great creative ideas, which is why good Media Buyers—either naturally or through training—learn the value of building and testing fantastic advertising that creates a strong customer click-through rate.

The methods and strategies in this book are responsible for hundreds of millions of dollars in sales. But it's not the recipe that makes a great chef. The question is whether you can harness what is given to you.

To be a great Media Buyer, you need to:
- Recognize a good idea and never turn one down
- Test it
- Recognize what you don't know
- Replicate your own version of great running ads
- Furthermore, you must believe that:
- Words are as strong as images

- Headlines are stronger than sub-headlines
- Sub-headings are stronger than body text
- The regular person is always your target
- Results are the necessity
- Not testing is failure

By this point you're already excited by the prospect of media buying, or you're completely bored. If you're bored by the idea of making millions, or the hard work you will have to do to get there, now is the time to put this book down and go about your business. There is nothing more for you here.

But if you're excited, then you may be a Media Buyer. If you are truly a Media Buyer at heart, I know I can only have your attention for a few hours; the remainder of this content is designed for you to digest in an afternoon.

Are You a Salesperson?

Yes. The answer can only be yes. Media buying is about creating convincing advertising targeted to consumers with known characteristics, *which makes them act*. That action is the sale. Media buying *is* sales.

But all life is sales and throughout life you will use negotiation, persuasion, and convincing. You want a spouse? Sell yourself. You want a job? Sell yourself. You want to go to University? Complete an application in which you sell yourself. If you're a parent, you probably realize that interactions with your children involve receiving constant sales pitches and countering them.

David Ogilvy says direct consumer marketing is the best of advertising: It's where the tire hits the pavement.[1] And I 100% agree with that. This means Media Buyers can come from disparate backgrounds, so long as they possess the attributes and drive that gains them the sales. Doormen, bartenders, medical professionals, people who love social media—the list of potentially great Media Buyers goes on and on. They come from all walks of life.

I have often tried to identify precisely what makes a Media Buyer and I've come up with this analogy: Identifying a Media Buyer is like having the ability to identify the sex of baby chicks.

Yes, baby chicks. Bear with me.

When chickens are hatched it's incredibly difficult to determine their sex. Yet in a hatchery, it's imperative to business to differentiate the males from females as efficiently and effectively as possible, moments after they're born. There are many ways to accomplish this feat, but the oldest and most effective method is for a person, a *chicken sexer*, to pick up the baby chicks, feel and touch each of them, and from this interaction intuitively categorize them as male or female. A good chicken sexer is 99.99% accurate.

How do they do it?

They work with someone who is already a chicken sexer and learn by watching, listening, and absorbing what the experienced chicken sexer does. After mere days of such mentorship, a person can learn to sex chickens in this way.

Identifying a Media Buyer is like chicken sexing with the added advantage of having a less embarrassing job title. And, while I don't know exactly how much a chicken sexer gets paid, I'm willing to bet it's not anywhere close to a million or more a year. At the end of the day, what I have learned is that the most accurate way to identify and develop a Media Buyer is to have someone experienced in the field work with them to see if they have the potential, and then, help them cultivate it.

The Dutch have a saying: "Is it better to be rich from someone else's good idea, or poor from your own bad idea?" To many it's an open question. The online space of direct-to-consumer marketing is still the Wild West. Amazon has major issues to address, such as fake review contamination. Real products are attacked by unscrupulous resellers in the countries where most products are made. Facebook is rife with bot traffic and fake accounts that pop up faster than mushrooms at midnight. And many unscrupulous Media Buyers cannibalize successful campaigns by taking the assets of others. Google and Facebook try to punish perpetrators with Artificial Intelligence (AI) that bans abusers, and instead often end up banning everyone involved—including the aggrieved party.

That said, watching what works and building something new on top of what is known is prudent practice, which I wholeheartedly endorse. *This is how we learn.*

Onward

I want you to succeed by reading from this book and learning all I have to tell you about my experiences with media buying, what works, and what doesn't. This is how you can begin your career.

If you read this book and digest its content, you will be in an excellent position to succeed as a Media Buyer, either employed by a company, or as an independent affiliate. You will learn to develop a Prime—an appeal that is unique to your product and helps propel it to profit. You will learn how to create a good, solid angle that will generate interest. You will understand how to use convincing copy and combine it with fantastic imagery. Most of all, you will put yourself in the mindset of the most successful Media Buyers in the world.

The great Media Buyers I know come from all walks of life. *You could be the next one.*

CHAPTER 2:

KNOW YOUR PRIME

I have written and run ads side by side with those of other writers. In the old world of catalogues and mail-order, results came back to us in six to eight weeks and you always had to be careful to wait for the last mail delivery before drawing any firm conclusions. We got results, but it was slow, and adapting wasn't easy.

In the online space, diverting one hundred to five hundred clicks to an A/B test is easy and fast. Results come in minutes, not weeks.

What consistently produces the winning headline or advertisement? The answer is simple: It's the *correct* appeal for that *particular* product or service.

I call this the "Prime."

Knowing your Prime is about asking what people want, understanding how they feel about what they want, and determining why they act on those wants.

Once you know what the Prime is, you can:

- Craft what consumers need
- Influence what they want
- Create an ad that is meaningful
- Satisfy them with the right product

The Prime is more like a quest to achieve than it is a single metric. It changes for each product and each audience.

Think about this: The goal of the advertising we work with is to make people act. Everything you write or create is in service of creating the action you desire. Although it may contain an opinion, performance marketing is not journalism. Although it may tell a story, it is not a novel. *It is designed to create an action.*

The Prime of the product is the guiding light that gets you there. But let's back up to the beginning because the Prime doesn't shine out of thin air.

We are discussing the Prime first because it's important to explain the intellectual framework—but remember that before you start to build and define your Prime, you need to acquire, test, and use the product.

Until you really understand the product, you can't create a winning Prime.

I recall building our team of product sources and developers in Hong Kong. When you are making millions of products you need someone who is thinking about the consumers and their needs and desires, and I interviewed an amazing young lady there who worked for my team for many years. She came from the adult toy business, and I was looking for someone to ensure quality control of our general merchandise and electronics. I asked her only one question: "Cheryl, how are you going to improve our quality control to ensure we deliver great products?"

She said, "Mr. Bruce, for the last ten years I have been going to China, opening boxes of dildos, taking samples, ensuring they have all certifications. In a room full of men, I have been examining them individually to ensure they are of the highest quality for people. I can handle your watches, electronics, and jewelry."

With that I knew to hire her: You need to boldly test and assess your wares to discern the Prime for what you are selling. Under no circumstance can you skip this step. You must know your product, including its specific quality, and certainly its benefits over all competition. You cannot be timid in finding out. One thing about adult toys I learned is that the *scent* of the materials is critical to customer adoption and satisfaction. Any top seller would need to know this detail; they would need to *find out.*

When you begin to write or create angles for your product or service, it's all about doing the research to *truly understand your product*. You need to create compelling words, not for the sake of reading but to elicit action from customers. Clicks and buys. To do this successfully: know the product, use the product, and get relevant people to try the product. Even try to break it, cut it open and look inside, push it to all its limits.

I personally spend a great deal of time just thinking about the product I intend to sell. I ruminate. What makes it unique? Where are the competitors, and where are there none? What keeps people from replicating this product, what makes it special? I distill my thoughts. I isolate and focus on a product's particular advantage, especially the *leading advantage*, which is the one that will turn an ordinary product into a best-seller.

The Prime of the product becomes the tool with which you will create the *headline*. The headline is the most important thing you will write. Without a great headline, the ship is sunk before it hits the harbor. *The headline is what makes people want to buy.*

Several years ago, when we started to look for products for direct-to-consumer retail, I was sitting in my office in Vancouver, where I was based at the time, just minutes before our hometown hockey team was about to take to the ice. I said to my staff, all of whom were millennials, "Let's watch the game on the TV in my office." They said we had no cable, so we couldn't watch it. I replied that we should get an antenna.

There was a bit of laughter and some smart-aleck remarks, "Boss, you can't watch TV with an antenna, what is this, the 1950's?"

But I was up for the challenge. I went to the local big-box electronics store and, with some searching, found an old-style TV antenna. I brought it back to the office and set it up. It worked. From then on, we were able to watch our team lose game after game, for free.

From there, our agency made the decision to create marketing that would bring back the old TV antenna. No joke, we did it. I spent a great deal of time with the product, thinking about its properties and design. We identified that the antenna is a very low-cost product that can come in many functional styles. It's incredibly easy to set up. Moreover, it provides exceptional access to local high-definition broadcasting. In fact, the quality of the picture picked up by the antenna is *better* than regular cable TV because the signal is not compressed. It helps you connect to products, such as TiVo, to help you skip the hassle of all those commercials bought by the old-school Media Buyers.

But the thing I *really* cared about was the antenna's single most important feature: You could pick up great television and not have to pay a huge cable bill every month.

This was the Prime. It was a fantastic one at that. "Cut the Cord" appealed to people, even millennials. Cable companies had spent the last thirty years convincing all of us that cable was the only way to watch

TV. Most people were shocked to learn they could use something so simple as an antenna to save thousands of dollars in their lifetime.

And thousands of dollars we did save them. We received many cease-and-desist letters falsely claiming that TV antennas were illegal, and we viewed them as the markers of success. We made the sales that put a dent in cable revenue.

All Roads Lead to the Prime

When I was a young trial lawyer, the very senior lawyer who trained me told me there were only two things to know if you wanted to win jury trials. First, make sure one juror is very pretty so you can stay awake and keep your attention on the trial (these weren't his exact words, but you get the point). Second, and most importantly, digest the case and stick to *one key aspect*. Then hammer that one aspect home, *over and over and over again.*

Why is this central theme, the defining aspect, so critically important not just to legal trials but to advertising?

It's because people want to:
- Be convinced
- Know the big reason
- Make a decision
- Feel good
- Have things easily explained

And all of these aspects must tie in together. This is why good stories, good jokes, and good copy have a certain pattern of repetition. It does not have to be formulaic, but it needs to flow from the big meaning—the Prime—and from that, you can create good headlines and good copy. Dave Chappelle, who is a poetically unfiltered comedic genius in his comedy specials, always has a way of bringing his audience back to right where he opened. You laugh, you respect his intelligence, and you feel satisfied with his close and stage walk-off. The key: don't save anything for later. There is no big reveal. You lead with the Prime and everything that follows is about the Prime. If it isn't, it won't mean anything to the reader.

Kurt Vonnegut offered us a list of rules about writing. The first rule was: "Use the time of a total stranger in such a way that he or she will not feel the time was wasted."[2] Although Vonnegut was a story writer talking about fiction, the sentiment is absolutely true in advertising. The split-second a customer gets the feeling their time is being wasted, you lose them.

The Prime is, in its essence, one simple, strong idea. It must have legs and it must apply to your product, carrying forward to other products and marketing. The concept, if properly framed, will become an industry-standard angle that gets adopted, reused, and rehashed.

To make the Prime powerful, you must express it *clearly* and *concisely*.

This means you have to use words in a very different way than you may have been taught before. The normal way to enhance a word, the way you may have picked up in school, involves cracking open a thesaurus (or searching the word in an online thesaurus) to find a fancy replacement as a method to enhance… In other words, you splay a lexicographic compendium, exhume an appellation that you are desirous of amendment, and appropriate the most Byzantine recapitulation you can divine!

At which point, honestly, someone should storm into your office, pull your underpants over your head, and break your glasses.

For a strong writer, language is a tool that's used to *make ideas clear*, never to complicate them. Make the words in your copy the ones that are simplest and hold the most emotional impact. Write not to the erudite sesquipedalian, but to any regular Joe or Jane who may come across your words. Choose words for simplicity and emotion. Complex words with multiple connotations are all but guaranteed to lose people. *Simple. Clear. Emotional.* It's that easy. And use the Prime, always, as your guiding force.

In short, shoot for the stars. You may not hit one every time but aiming high always beats aiming low. The Prime allows you to sharpen that arrow and aim it. The Prime is how you hit the heart of the consumer.

Critically, the Prime in media buying allows you to:

- Focus your headline
- Focus your choice of images

- Make your statement powerful
- Focus the rest of your copy
- Make all your assets relevant

Failing to adopt the Prime leads only to disaster. You will be at work without a central theme, forced to Frankenstein together unrelated and weak ideas in a futile attempt to create a powerful one. This approach will surely lead you to a fate similar to Dr. Frankenstein's monster: "Borne away by the wave and lost in darkness and distance."[3]

Accept that finding the one, central Prime is *critical* to developing your advertising. Furthermore, accept that the clearer and simpler the basis, the more appealing it is.

Do not fall into the trap of taking this one Prime angle and machine-gunning it with multiple repeats of the same copy or words. Keep your work clear, simple, condensed, entertaining, and targeted. Otherwise, you will slide down the slippery slope to bad marketing.

What makes bad marketing?

Simple. If it doesn't make people buy, it's bad. It can be entertaining, it can be artistic, it can be beautiful, perhaps it will even win an award in some "best advertising" category—but in my opinion if it doesn't compel people to purchase the product, it's bad. Certainly, this is the case for performance marketing.

The sad reality is that the majority of advertising does *not* do anything substantial. So, how do we solve this?

The Importance of Testing

Now you know: In media buying, you must focus your efforts on perfecting the Prime. To achieve the Prime, you can't be afraid to test your ideas. Any idea could be a contender. And remember, *you must never turn down a good idea.*

But how do you know which are the good ones? How do you narrow down the good ideas to select the best focus, the Prime?

The answer is always in *testing*. To find the Prime, build ads with various possible Primes and do some A/B testing. For this testing, you can actually use people online to find out what your audience responds to. You can empirically determine what people *think* is the Prime—and then set to hammering it home.

Never forget that everything changes; advertising is in constant flux. Online is the fastest-changing workplace in history. What worked yesterday may not work today, what works today may not work tomorrow. Speed that up, moment-to-moment in some cases, because this is the fast-paced world we live and work in.

For example, take Amazon buttons: It used to be the standard belief that green was the best responsive color for buttons. Yet Amazon proved, through market research and sales results, that the most responsive color for buttons is, in fact, orange. Don't be surprised if in a few years, a few months even, after new testing or changes in culture or audience, the color has gone back to green. Or maybe the color changes entirely. Make way for purple...

In short, the online market is fluid, its audience is fluid, and so your responses to it must also be fluid. The Prime is the central idea and the focus for the Media Buyer's work. The right Prime must be arrived at and used to your full advantage. Testing the audience will help you find the Prime. Knowing the Prime will make you money.

For real results, you must test properly. This requires a basic understanding of statistics. Remember: size matters. We all know that if you flip a coin the chance of it landing on heads is 50% and tails is 50% too. But if you were to toss a coin four times, there is only a 38% chance you would get heads twice. The closer you get to an infinite number, the higher the likelihood that you see 50% heads and 50% tails.

The general rule is that the more precise the information you're testing, the larger the sample size you want. We are fortunate enough in this day and age as performance marketers to have easy access to relatively large numbers of subjects when testing. The general rule is that you want to make use of as large a sample size as you can get in a short amount of time. Too small, and your test is worthless. But you don't need to wait for a million clicks to get a reliable outcome. A sample is meant to be representative of a population; it is not the population in its entirety.

I can think of literally dozens and dozens of stories related to testing and retesting and being surprised at the result. I love reading books on testing just to generate new concepts for testing from old ideas. I often work with DFO Global's Chief Analytics Officer, Timur Shuvaloff, who has been amazing at building and executing tests and putting the results to great use. Having come from print media, I have a certain view of how marketing should look. I love to see stamps and seals and the "official look." Tim is a minimalist and we're always friendly debating the two styles.

I recall making a warranty for him to test on an electronic product called Infinitikloud. Timur was advocating for a very simple, elegant, non-decorated warranty page. I had the art department make up a warranty certificate with swirly borders and gold seals and stamps, bold headings, and the dramatic appearance of a stock certificate. When I showed Timur he laughed and said it was the most gaudy, tasteless look he could imagine. He was right—but it also looked official and dramatic.

We made a friendly wager on which look would out-perform the other. Remember, the copy was identical. We ran the A/B test, and Timur ran into my office saying, "I cannot believe that cheesy looking warranty page beat my beautiful elegant version!"

Timur stated two things, which I think are important, and which we have followed since. First, marginal gains are okay, but when doing testing—go for and seek the big gains. Second, don't judge solely by the look, as different target demographics respond in different ways. It turns out the purchasers of that particular Infinitikloud product were significantly older than Timur had anticipated—more my age, people accustomed to the look of print media.

Testing is also about mathematics. Make sure you really have the correct sample size. When you get results, you want fast action—but make sure your sample is truly representative.

We launched a big test that was highly successful based on a twenty-sale sample. One item had six conversions and the other had fourteen. The winner, initially, was clear, and due to it being a media buying test, we cut it early and took our result as a win. Excited, we rolled out the product to take advantage. Yet over time, we found the result wasn't sticking—if anything, it actually *reduced* conversion rates. When we re-ran the test using a larger sample, we found that the initial results were simply an anomaly, like flipping a coin twenty times and getting fourteen heads. We did not have enough conversions and learned a valuable lesson. No matter how exciting the initial results seem, work the math and seek statistical significance.

I love testing and if you are going to be a Media Buyer you will also embrace and love testing. Testing is beautiful because, based on your results, you get to know whether to make a change in the marketing, or change nothing. If the answer is to change nothing, your task is to come up with another test to beat the original, and then to beat that. The process is eminently challenging.

One thing that you need to be careful of is "the new person tail chase." This happens when you get a new person on the marketing team and they say, for example, "Amazon has orange call to action buttons, but ours are green! We need to test orange call to action buttons!" So, you test, and low and behold the orange buttons seem to out-perform the existing green buttons. Then the new person says, "Apple call to action buttons are blue! Let's test blue!" And low and behold, the blue buttons beat the orange buttons. So, you change everything to blue. Then: "Wow the Kardashians with Shopify are using green buttons," and you test, and guess what? We're back to the original color.

Don't chase testing that doesn't need to be done. The reality of buttons is they're more complicated than the singularity of a color choice. The issues are complex and pose questions such as, does the button stand out of the palette of the website, does the button capture the emotion of the brand?

Over time you will develop your own sense of intuition into what works. Or, if you don't, you can partner up with or work alongside someone who possesses this ability. While intuition doesn't eliminate the need for testing, your instincts or good opinions will tell you what to test for and help you define your testing strategy. Testing is an important tool, but don't become a slave to testing the patently obvious.

CHAPTER 3:

KNOW YOUR PRODUCT

The Prime you choose depends on both the context for the marketing and your target consumer. The goal is always to encourage consumers to buy and then buy some more, or to get them to use more of the product or service you're selling. You need sales and more sales to bring in the money.

I suppose if you were really bad at this then the more advertising you did, the less consumers would purchase. Eventually, unless you were selling a price-inelastic good that relied on minuscule sales, you'd have a dead business. Assuming you seek sales, that you want your advertiser's bank account full—moreover that you expect to be paid a hefty commission for your work as you *increase* the volume of sales—read on.

Selecting your Prime starts with knowing *everything* about your product.

I do not and cannot start crafting the Prime until I have spent a lot of time with the product. I hold it, take it apart, use it as intended, and use it for a variety of things for which it was not intended. This is where creativity kicks in and ideas can form. I want to test the product's limits, to break it open, see what makes it tick.

That, for me, is the fun bit—but the actual research on the product is essential. If you don't do your research, you can quickly go down the wrong path. Or perhaps, at times, you'll find out that you shouldn't be buying media for this product at all.

Research the business owners, check the patents and trademarks. Make sure what you are selling is real and see what you can learn from knowing where it came from. Then, find the comparable competitor products and see what they're doing differently.

At this point, it's nice to be senior, as I will often task a junior person to dig up the dirt on a product and its competitors. But you can only delegate so much. Media Buyers who are not willing to read and are not either self-educated or otherwise educated, make me nervous. If I ask, "How are you coming up with the assets?" and their answer is simply, "Gut feeling," or "My ideas," or "Creativity," I become very skeptical, very fast.

Know your competitor's product. Line up their products alongside your own and put them to the test. Learn what works and what doesn't; discover how your product functions in relation to the competitor's product. *Knowing where your product stands against competition helps you define your Prime.*

Media buying is not only about building ad sets, making marketing, and buying traffic. There is a skill and science associated with discerning what offer should be worked on. Not all offers are created equal, and there are things you can do as a Media Buyer to identify if an offer has scalability on conversion. These factors impact your ability to buy traffic and to scale that traffic because traffic sources want to ensure you are building their reputation rather than diminishing it.

Consider the following:

- **Product Reputation** is critical to scalability. Products with controversial images or in controversial categories will find that the major traffic sources set up roadblocks to high volume purchases. Traffic sources assess a product's reputation by polling their customers and allowing feedback on the ads or types of ads they're being served.

- **Intellectual Property (IP) Protection** is a mark of the advertiser's investment in their product and provides your ability to ensure that a bunch of copycat offers do not come in to steal your advertising for a competitor project. If you have a choice between a product without IP or with IP protection, always go with the IP protected product. *What do you look for?* Patents. Is there a utility patent or design patent on the product? A utility patent prevents anyone else from selling something with the same function, and a design patent can stop other companies from selling something with the same design. Trademarking also helps protect you by stopping unauthorized companies from selling under the same name.

Be ready for anything. Doing the research is mandatory and an ongoing endeavor because you never know when a new product will come out with features that are more advanced, or at least different from yours. Be prepared to respond if someone tries to beat you to the marketing punch by staying informed. Good marketing research helps you anticipate change.

Media Buying is a profession, and much of what works in advertising has been predetermined. There is a wealth of great information and research you should draw from. I love to hear statements from Media Buyers such as, "I'm reading old ads," or "I read ten hours' worth of competitive research," or "I'm in the middle of a new book about advertising, or motivation, or consumer behavior."

Imagine your wife is about to have a baby and during the epidural the doctor says, "Hey! I just thought up a new creative way to insert the needle!" *Just imagine it.*

Is this what you want to hear from an expert? Is it even close to what you want to hear? I sure wouldn't, and neither would my wife (or anyone else's). Such a doctor should have his medical license taken away.

The sure path to failure is "winging it" without putting in the time and effort to learn what's already out there and what can and should be done to achieve sales. Build up your creativity on a basis of research and product knowledge. Media buying is a science: always logical and strategic. Learn from other more experienced Media Buyers *before* you put money on the line. Watch and see how it is done.

Also, always remember that you are not necessarily the *same* as your customer. You may have great taste, varied interests, and a keen sense of the fantastic—but that doesn't mean your dream product will sell well. Products that sell the best hold broad appeal and target a wide potential consumer group. Performance marketing is not the place for niche products. Bear in mind that just because something is of interest to you personally, doesn't mean it's destined for best-seller.

The Key to Selling

The key to selling is to truly understand your product and the market it's situated in. The more you know about the product, the more you will work toward the Prime. Remember that the Prime is the ultimate, the best theme from which to create your ad work; it is the "Cut the Cable" of antenna sales.

The product you're marketing must be at the center of the advertising when we are working direct-to-consumer. We often talk about the hero section of an online ad, that space old-schoolers call "above the fold." The hero is the first thing a consumer will see, so all the information here must be clear, concise, and compelling—moreover, it must be understood visually. This is where your Prime must be most clearly articulated.

Consider the old parable: A group of six blind men who have never seen an elephant encounter one for the first time. The first blind man remarks on what a strange animal it is, he grabs the trunk and says it's very much like a snake. The second blind man reaches out and finds a flapping ear and says the elephant is like a fan. The third grabs a leg and says it's as sturdy as a tree. The fourth touches the belly and says it's like a wall one could not pass. The fifth grabs its tail and says it's like a rope used for climbing. The final man, near the front of the elephant, feels the tusk and describes it as a weapon, much like a spear.

The meaning behind the parable is that various bits and pieces make up the whole. As it relates to media buying, the hero section is where you showcase the entire product, which yes, can later be highlighted according to its various attributes—but here is the product displayed as complete and desirable. You, more than anyone else, must be the expert on this. You should be able to craft a strong hero section so that your customer knows as much as you do about the product *in as little time as possible*. You must flash them the whole elephant, not just its parts.

Another adage to make the point: Sell the sizzle, not the steak (although I hope tenderloin comes along with that sizzle).

You cannot sell what you do not show to the customer. If you are selling a pig, show the pig. The pig does not need lipstick or a dress. Feature the product correctly and in the best possible light, which is defined by your Prime and nothing more. *It is the Prime that is the sizzle.*

There will be nothing boring about your product because if you find its Prime, you have the key to unlocking its marketing. All products can be boring on their own: Products do not sell themselves until you build the Prime.

Further to your own knowledge of the product, consider the customer's knowledge of it and any existing connections that can be made. This understanding of the relationship between customer and product is very valuable. There are three basic scenarios you will come across with unique considerations for each: new customer, known product; new customer, new product; and known customer, known product.

New Customer, Known Product

If the product is known to the consumer, it has an existing emotional impact you can tap into. The Prime and angles to known products are usually established and clear. In most cases, you are best served to carry them forward. For example, why launch New Coke when Coke Classic has a great emotional connection, stretches back generations, and has successfully sold millions of Cokes?

New Customer, New Product

If you have a new product or brand that isn't well-known, you don't have the canned materials or trusted brand guidelines to assist you. This can be an exciting time for marketing; you will need to research and understand the product and discover what new emotional ties can be created.

Known Customer, Known Product

If you have previously sold someone a good quality product, this is your dream customer. What happens now is called remarketing. You can sell them more of the same, and then an improved widget, an upgrade, and more. For example, selling more Apple products to Apple users is easier than taking candy from a baby (as the saying goes, perhaps not literally true). In the mail order and catalogue world, we called repeat purchasers "multis" or "multi-buyers." They were coveted customers, and everyone dreamed of cultivating more.

Consider that selling a TV antenna to a Comcast customer may be an easy task, but upselling a Comcast customer to a service plan, well… maybe not. When remarketing to a known customer who has previously bought the product, you must intimately know the ups and downs of the product and take advantage of knowing your customer.

In the case of remarketing, it is important to gauge and work with the existing emotional tie to the product and the particular need that it fills. Become familiar with the opinions of your customer in deciding on the primary way to reach them. Remarketing should follow closely what the customers are saying in online reviews. Your customer service team will be an effective support and can help address customer pain points for better decisions down the road, as well as upsells.

Retargeting is what happens when a previously targeted customer has heard your pitch and engaged with your advertising—but not yet made the purchase. In the case of retargeting, you are bringing them back to hear the Prime.

When a customer must be retargeted, it can be a mistake to think you need to alter the Prime to make the sale. Resist that urge! Recognize and respect the Prime concept for your advertising. We aren't reinventing the wheel here; rather, we are using the *right* wheel for the *right* application.

If you look back at other advertising campaigns, you will see the path to the Prime; when you have that, stick with it. Coke, for example, knew their Prime. Coke is Classic. But in a catastrophic move, they almost destroyed it when they introduced New Coke. This shattered the image of an existing product, effectively undercutting their own Prime. Not only did they fail to sell New Coke, they nearly fatally damaged their existing brand. It was only thanks to the strength of the original Prime that Coke managed to return to it and avert total disaster.

If you have found the Prime, you have your best marketing at hand. You have your guiding theme and hold the key to the sale: Don't change the Prime to re-engage the customer. Instead, condense and make the path to purchase even easier.

You will have buyers that leave your ads but are still interested in finding your product. These people end up in the search engines, looking around for your product again. And they will actually make it back to your pages *if those pages are properly indexed for the search.*

Thus, you need to carefully select what marketing you let the large search engines index—so that these customers can find you again.

If you are running paid ads and have interesting copy, you will get as high as 25% of people who view your ad in the category I call "falloff." Falloff happens when you pay a provider for traffic and your advertising sparks an interest. The consumer then puts your product name in a search engine, and from there it's up to *your content* to pave the path back to your product and the sale.

Falloff contains amazing buyer potential because these are people who are now actively researching your ad.

In anticipation of falloff, you will want Google to find your path. You will have indexed it correctly to assist with this. Additionally, you will have created or used funnel sites to gather in these searches and bring these customers back to your pages for purchase.

Predicting a Prime with longevity and emotional power is the key to creating a product that will sell to customers, new and old. No product is sold without marketing. Products that simply roll out of bed and sell themselves are figments of our imagination; in reality, the only way we can succeed is by finding the Prime.

You must find the Prime and hold onto it to retarget and regain falloff. What are the possible ways you know you have found the Prime?

Well, the Prime is:

- Succinctly expressed in words
- Still amazing the next day
- Formed in a state of focus, in the flow
- A team or group idea *so good* you wish it was yours alone
- A feeling of timeless emotional connection

Never forget: The Prime is imperative to the context for your marketing and for targeting the customer.

In Summation

The Prime is born of your complete and total understanding of the product, and mindful of its reflexive relationship to the context and consumer. You will hook

your customers with the Prime. You will keep them and
bring them back to complete the sale.

CHAPTER 4:

WORD YOUR PRIME

The words you use to express your Prime are critical to engaging customers. You can have the best Prime idea in the history of advertising, but if no one can tell what it is, you may as well have nothing.

The key task is to take a good solid product and build headlines and copy that communicate effectively and are *meaningful* to the Prime of the product. Consider some amazing examples of Primes expressed in the taglines of famous copy and let them help guide you.

Hitting the Mark

Budweiser: The King of Beers

The Prime makes this beer so elite it emits a notion of royalty. It creates an image in our mind of majestic Budweiser, far superior to any other beer. The King of Beers is the Prime because beer is otherwise a commonplace beverage, not associated with princes, kings, and queens. Yet with the Prime, in the minds of the consumer they become members of the elite—simply by popping open a nice cold Bud.

Gillette: The Best A Man Can Get

There is only so much you can say about shaving your face, yet who knew it could make you a better version of yourself? With this Prime, Gillette has fused a man's desire to be better, to be the best, even, simply by using their product. It's not just the best *product* a man can buy; the product makes him the best man he can *be*.

Who wouldn't crave that?

Hallmark: When You Care Enough to Send the Very Best

This Prime elicits an emotional response. "When you care enough to send the very best" signifies to the consumer that if you *don't* choose Hallmark, you don't *actually* care about your loved ones. At very least, you don't care enough.

Are you the sort of person who puts in a half-effort when it comes to recognizing the ones you love? Or are you the sort to truly *care?* Which is it? Choose one!

Wheaties: Breakfast of Champions

The Prime conveys that the very act of eating Wheaties puts you in a league with the mightiest of athletes, the champs. This is reinforced by the use of the winningest, most well-known athletes—including Super Bowl champions and world record holders—on the packaging.

You can be a champion too, of course, if you eat your Wheaties.

De Beers: A Diamond is Forever

Believe it or not, the diamond engagement ring was not always the obvious, go-to ritual it has become. Following the Great Depression and then the Second World War, diamond sales cratered, and diamond miners like De Beers were in trouble. Then, in 1947, a copywriter named Frances Gerety came up with the tagline "A Diamond is Forever," which has been used in every single De Beers engagement ad since.[4] Clearly a winning Prime.

Crest: Look Ma, No Cavities!

Toothpaste was never going to be glamorous. You use it for one main reason: to keep your teeth from rotting out of your head. But that's not exactly an appealing angle. With this Prime, Crest was able to convey the benefit of their product and add in the extra, age-old benefit of pleasing one's mother. Or, more accurately, given that mothers would be the primary buyers of toothpaste, convey what mothers hoped to hear—perfectly appealing to the consumer's desire.

7-Up: The Uncola

The Prime: 7-Up is everything that colas are *not*. Clear, crisp, and clean. How refreshing. How badly do you want it now?

Make 7-UP Yours

The British Prime for 7-Up: An irreverent concept, perhaps one only the British truly appreciate, which tells that the beverage is one-of-a-kind and worthy of consumption—*by you*. Note that geographic and cultural differences can subtly shift the Prime.

Visa: It's Everywhere You Want to Be

This is a Prime that literally promises you the world. And in its context, it delivers on it.

Milton Glaser: I ♥ NY

Perhaps the best and most elegant Prime of Milton Glaser, a true genius who captured the heart and love of the amazing city. Everyone loves New York and feels compelled to display that love.

Missing It

Yet not all Prime making has been so savvy. Some advertisers badly missed their mark, failed to find the Prime, and as a result, failed to effectively advertise their product.

Failed Primes can have disastrous results for your brand and product. In some cases, they can be the death of it.

There are many poorly conceived Primes that have left brands in a worse position than if they had done no advertising at all. With hindsight, it is easy to see why they failed, but you really have to wonder what they were thinking when they decided to go ahead with the Primes that missed their mark.

Craven A: Will Not Affect Your Throat

Perhaps an innocent lie, but this attempt at a Prime was most certainly derived from understanding consumer concerns and the association of smoking with the "smoker's cough." It was a great assurance on a rather evil product, and in the end, we all know how much harm lighting up can actually do to our throats. Reminding people of this unfortunate reality of smoking was a dodgy move by Craven A.

Bloomingdales: Spike Your Best Friend's Eggnog When They are Not Looking

Bloomingdales ended up apologizing for it. I'm not sure they made any true effort here to find their Prime.

This feels like the sort of tagline someone came up with in an attempt at being edgy and clever, but without having any understanding of what they were selling, or to whom they were selling it. Add in deceit and treachery, and ask yourself, for what gain?

Know your product, know your consumer, and know the context: this advice is fundamental.

Uzbekistan Airways: Good Luck

This one sort of speaks for itself and I'd like to hope something got lost in translation as an explanation. The result is a very bad Prime, which means it isn't really a Prime. Air travel might be dangerous, so how about some *luck* to make it through? You can just picture the shrug that accompanies the sentiment. This one isn't selling flights.

Budweiser: The Perfect Beer for Removing No from Your Vocabulary for the Night

When the "King of Beers" went from royalty to street thug... Did it cross their minds that they were suggesting the word for *consent* should be removed? Does any beer want the reputation of cancelling out good judgment?

Cremo Cigars: There's No Spit in Cremo

Why would anyone think that there is? Even when trying to counteract a spread of misinformation, if the best benefit you can dream up to convey quality is that no one has spit in your product, you haven't tried hard enough. Or at all. This is not a Prime, it's a suicide note.

Cherry Dr. Pepper: It's Not for Women

Hard to tell if this is an example of a bad Prime (the idea that Cherry Dr. Pepper is tied to masculinity), or if they didn't bother to come up with a Prime in the first place. I kind of suspect the latter. This one made a lot of people mad, and it didn't sell soda.

Reebok: Cheat on Your Girlfriend, Not Your Workout

Reebok misunderstood its brand or had a Nike copywriter with a concussion create this Prime that wasn't a Prime. They played with the idea of "good cheating" which is inevitably morally questionable. Most brands should not want to be associated with poor choices, and most consumers do not want to mentally associate themselves with immoral behavior. Steer clear.

The Good, the Bad, and Your Prime

These examples are fairly extreme, and I would expect that you would have the sense to learn from the good and avoid any of the obviously bad ones. But in the middle, there exists a vast desert of pseudo-Primes, which are neither great nor terrible. They are nothing; they do nothing and sell nothing.

Which brings us to a consideration of basic human psychology in relation to writing the Prime. When we market, we draft and word our Prime to suit the recipient, their needs and desires. Always consider: How will the product change the customer's life for the better? How will the product solve a persistent problem not yet solved?

Fundamentally: How might your ad *create* the problem, then offer your product as the solution?

Your Prime doesn't need to go down in history alongside "I 🩶 NY." But it needs to drive sales, and it needs to speak to people.

How you write about your Prime must invoke *what people want*. Always return to an understanding of base needs and desires, the same for all people. Some particular British flare aside, on a basic human level, needs and wants are shared across cultures. This is why great advertising ports between countries and transverses the globe.

The Significance of Maslow's Hierarchy

Desire for specific products depends on various happenings in a consumer's life at any given moment in time, and yet always relates to Maslow's hierarchy.

Maslow's hierarchy is a ranking of needs and wants and a way of explaining what motivates people to seek out goals.[5] In our case, the goals can be understood as products and services. Though the hierarchy is often expressed in terms of the visual pyramid, it is accepted amongst advertisers that a customer's motivations can operate on multiple levels at the same time, or in varying degrees. And you can see differing media providers speaking to different levels of the hierarchy.

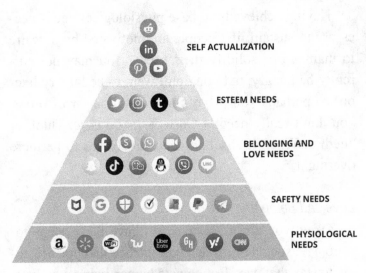

MEDIA ON MASLOW'S HIERARCHY

Figure 2. Media on Maslow's Hierarchy.

Next, let's consider each rank in Maslow's Hierarchy as it relates to media buying.

The Physiological

These are our most basic needs. Until these needs are met, we are unlikely to spend much time worrying about anything else. These most basic of human needs transcend all cultures. The degree to which the physiological motivates people will vary, but it is common to all. A good example is Dasani's "Can't live without it" water branding.

Safety and Security

Having achieved the base physiological needs necessary to sustain life, people are motivated by a desire to maintain or solidify their needs. You may not currently be hungry, but you don't want to be hungry later on, so perhaps you'll buy the two-gallon jar of olives you don't really need at Costco, *just in case*. Think of "FedEx. When it absolutely, positively has to be there overnight."

Love and Belonging

Okay, you are alive, and you have taken steps toward a reasonable degree of confidence that you are going to stay that way. But being a human being, you have a strong desire to hold a place of belonging alongside other human beings. You want friendships, intimacy, family. You don't want to be outcast, and you don't want to be alone. Remember Nokia: "Connecting People."

Self-Esteem

This is where Freud's concept of the ego comes into play. People don't just want to belong; they want to feel good about themselves. They want others to feel good about them too. Status, respect, importance, and recognition are key components. Consider: "BMW. The Ultimate Driving Machine."

Self-Actualization

The desire to live at one's full potential rests at the top of our motivations and is understood to be the end result of achieving the previous levels. The US Army best captures the essence of self-actualization with "Be All That You Can Be."

Taken Together

These five levels of the hierarchy are the base factors that drive all humans to action. Essential to the Media Buyer is both a knowledge of the basic elements and a variety of sub-desires that impact them. If the purpose of an ad is to create an action, then you must understand what motivates people to act. Maslow doesn't offer a perfect model, but his pyramid is a good starting place for understanding what prompts people to act.

There are other subcategories of motivational impulses that are particularly relevant in the world of direct marketing. These include the desire to:

- Know more than your neighbor
- Satisfy curiosity
- Save resources
- Acquire an easy, dependable resolution to a complex issue
- Express a solution to a problem to others

Finally, we're left with pain versus pleasure. Perhaps this is a sad comment on the state of our world today, but the reality is as such: people buy things to address the problem of pain and the pursuit of pleasure. And relief or avoidance of pain tends to sell *significantly better* than pursuit of pleasure. Pain is the more immediate and motivating of the duo; pain is about today and yesterday, whereas pleasure is about tomorrow. So, in light of Maslow, perhaps this is not surprising. Each product will have its own relationship to pain (or pleasure), and the better you understand it, the better your copy invokes it in the customer, and the more you will sell.

Flowing Toward More

The words you write need to take advantage of all of these needs as they relate to the consumer's engagement with the product. The best copy addresses human needs in a way that is immediately relatable to the consumer. Efficient, clear, concise writing that evokes a response: this is the goal.

Consider the COVID-19 pandemic. Previously, most affluent purchasers were not particularly concerned with the physiological level of the pyramid. Typically, if you wanted to sell to them you would create and word your Prime around the two top levels of the pyramid, targeting self-esteem and self-actualization. This changed rapidly, almost overnight, at the onset of the world-wide pandemic, and we began to see Primes worded toward basic survival. *What happened?* People's motivations changed, that's what happened.

Media buying offers an incredible ability to focus your advertising to specific groups. The Prime is an aspect of the personality of your product built for both the product and the target group together. People will be drawn to the product that fits their brand image, but sometimes they need to be educated as to what that image is.

Targeting on Google allows you to target by keywords in search of an audience. Facebook lets you create an audience, which becomes your target market. You can target very generally or very specifically using these online tools. Targeting includes building audiences around age, location, gender, job title, and more.

Writing to express the Prime is consistently mindful of not just the stagnant concept of "target audience," but a flow toward more. The flow holds a notion of audience-building, of expanding sales to more and more people, and this always happens with words.

CHAPTER 5:

DEVELOP YOUR ANGLE, YOUR HOOK

The angle for your marketing is the unifying concept you use to pitch the product to your customer. If you think of the Prime as an essence, think of the angle as your delivery tool.

The characteristics of the product impact how you define your marketing. Think long and hard about the specific product and the research that you have prepared. Think about how it relates to other products and what makes a person buy it.

Ask these questions:
- Is the product mature or new?
- Is the product simple or complex?
- Is the product a luxury item or basic need?
- Is the product something to be proud of or to own privately?
- Is the product an improvement on an existing item or original?

Coming up with the correct angle based on your Prime is essential to turning that retired accountant from New Jersey who happened to see your Facebook ad into a repeat customer who comes back for more. *How do you do that?*

First, understand what your customers can acquire, or have acquired. Determine who your target customer is by looking at other similar products sold on the market.

Know the competitor's Prime and work to understand these potential customers.

Know the competitor's angles. If there are competitors, it's a battle for customers. How are they advertising? How can you defeat their ads with lower cost bids and better performing pages, which naturally reduce the costs of media?

See what your competitors have that performs well and build advertising and creative assets that are a step ahead.

Consider how you frame your product. Take bottled water as an example. This is an entirely mundane purchase. What is being sold is something you can already get, essentially for free. But if you look at all the different brands of bottled waters out there (and bottled water is a roughly $300 billion a year industry) they are each framed differently. Each business has come up with a different angle for selling water, and the success of their product rests almost entirely on that.

Sometimes the angles for the Prime come directly from consumers. Our agency, Amasa, develops many fantastic cutting-edge marketing campaigns and has great experience with continuity type programs. Colgate, in particular the teeth whitening division, began working with us. Their Prime was clear. Colgate has been the lead in developing for consumers and has dominated space since the late 1880's. They were, however, feeling the pressure of newer direct-to-consumer brands built on a continuity model and social media. The angles that had been developed and used successfully were all taken by the Amasa team, focusing on the user-generated content that already existed. They understood that a great source of angles are customer service and consumer online postings of unboxing, talking about wine and coffee stain removal, and testimonials of the shade lighting effect of the Colgate products.

Funneling Customers

The current theory driving successful media buying is to push customers through a funnel from the media source to the purchase. Think of the funnel imagery: wide to narrow. I will talk about building funnels in detail later, but for now you just need to know a bit about them.

As an example, consider Facebook newsfeed ads. Using Facebook algorithms and specific organization, these ads target audiences and push traffic. What usually performs best, especially if the product is relatively unknown to the user, is to send them first to an *advertorial*. David Ogilvy did not create the concept, but he repeatedly purported the benefits of advertisements that appear like a news report about a product, and the effect that this approach lends to increasing sales. The advertorial looks official and appears to objectively educate the consumer on both their problem and a lack of great solutions for solving it; furthermore, the advertorial lets the consumer know about a product that can solve their problem better than any other option on the market ever could. For those not familiar, David Ogilvy summarizes the advertorial as having the look and feel of a news article that reports on issues surrounding the product or service.[6] Despite its newsworthy appearance, the advertorial is, of course, the marketing itself, and you must create it. It should go without saying: the advertorial will hammer home the Prime.

The headline is the most important part of the advertorial. Most people don't read the full article, they just skim it. It's critical to call out the key points in bold, not to write in big blocks of text, and to keep the article very "stream of consciousness" in style. Advertorials are usually best written in the first- or second-person voice, often taking the form of a personal account of using a product.

From a convincing advertorial, the consumer is normally pushed to a more condensed page, which is called the *interstitial*. This type of page has narrowed the subject to become more streamlined on the product itself. Interstitials provide transitional advertising that focuses consumers on their need for the product and provide general value by keeping consumers engaged.

From the interstitial, consumers are directed to the *checkout*. To recap: At this point, the person has clicked on an interesting ad or video, read an advertorial informing them about the product or service in a newsworthy way, read an interstitial that's increasingly focused them on the problem and solution at hand, and is now very aware of the Prime. You have essentially turned the consumer into an expert on your product, all in under an hour. So, you put the checkout in front of them and let them make their decision, but don't over-sell.

E-COMMERCE FUNNEL

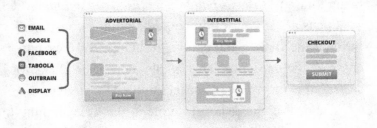

Figure 3. The e-commerce funnel from source to checkout.

All About Angles

Your Prime will help you define angles or hooks, which are used to grab the attention of your customer. There are a variety of different angle or hook strategies that you can use to put the Prime in motion. Each has a different purpose and can suit a certain audience or product type.

The most common strategies used to develop angles will offer a deal, solve the problem, shock or scare, or tell a story. These can be used individually or in combination with specific considerations for each.

The Deal

This is the straightforward pitch. Oftentimes, the Media Buyer has no control over the deal because it is determined by the advertiser, or the person building the checkout.

The checkout is usually where you will see discounts, clickable coupons, and deals for buying in bundles. If the checkout or website offers a deal, of course you can use that aspect in the advertising—the point being to use it *if it will pull people through the funnel*.

Focus all of your efforts here on pulling consumers through the funnel, the end result being that they purchase at the checkout. This is the concept of clicks to sales that is imperative to successful media buying.

The deal is the easiest to write in that it is straightforward marketing. It can perform very well, but it is perhaps the least elegant approach. Note: If your first idea to sell a product is to discount it or offer one free for each unit purchased, you have not really developed the Prime.

Solve the Problem

The truth is that a consumer usually doesn't care about the product itself. They do care about their various daily problems. Thus, the product as the *solution to those problems* is always a golden sales angle.

Consumers are often oblivious to new and trending products, and yet they live with the same problems every day. Can you identify any and all possible problems to associate with a product?

There are some savvy ways to get insight into consumer problems specific to products. If the project is mature, as in the product has been sold for some time and garnered feedback, go directly to customer service and see what people are saying about the product. Find out from existing customers how it solves or does not solve their problem.

Take this golden information to refocus and hone your Prime, to directly address and engage with the issues that get defined by consumers. Perhaps new issues came up with your product, which you weren't aware of when you were first researching it. Some products have added bonuses: They solve problems we didn't know the consumer had, which we weren't even aware the product could solve! Existing customers provide ongoing testing of the product. Having these consumer insights is always useful.

Shock or Negative Sale

The negative sale involves convincing people to buy a product based on shock and awe or fear. It is a common tactic that was further developed with the COVID-19 pandemic. Shock or awe can offer strong motivators to consumers, particularly for impulse purchases. That said, I have a few problems with negative angles.

First, many people who impulse buy based on momentary shock created via an advertisement may find that their motivation reverses as the shock wears off. At this point, they experience buyer's remorse. Buyer's remorse matters to you as a Media Buyer because your ideal scenario involves positive feedback and repeat customers.

Second, fear is often situational and can resolve itself in time. You'll be in trouble as a Media Buyer if you don't work to develop a long-lasting campaign. Think about New Coke again if you need an example of what not to do.

Third, negative sales can feel predatory and profiteering. They can attach negative images and ideals to the concept of the product and ought to be carefully balanced.

In my opinion, only go negative when the product solves a negative problem. If the consumer is likely to be worried about an issue long-term—the shock is not simply based on a trending news article—you may want to go negative because long-term concerns would be addressed. The shock would not wear off in these cases, and the consumer would likely not experience buyer's remorse; rather, they would use the product in an ongoing manner. Theoretically, they could become repeat customers.

A thought exercise: How might a mask sold during the COVID-19 pandemic be marketed in such a way that it offers long-term problem-solving and becomes a repeat purchase, even as the COVID-19 issue is resolved?

The Story

The story is the classic method to engage a consumer. Everyone loves a story. Story is how we share our culture, learn our language, come into being, and even how we create the way we see ourselves.

A compelling story entwines the interest of the customer with the product. Product and consumer are linked by narrative. Story is the oldest angle one can choose, and if properly told, it garners strong interest in the product, resulting in sales.

When buying media, a story is best told consistently from the first asset to the checkout. The story needs to be logical and needs to flow naturally from advertorial to interstitial to checkout. The story paves these transitions and guides the consumer down the path.

Failing to be consistent with the story, or presenting inconsistent facts within it, makes your entire pitch less believable. The creative assets must lead in and flow to one another; they ought to feel both entertaining and inevitable, building excitement for what's coming in the next step just as in a good movie or novel you wouldn't want to put down.

Build Ad Sets for Targeting

No matter which angle you go with, the media must have certain characteristics. The media must be:

- Relevant to the end product or service being sold, not simply clickbait
- Consistent in fact and style
- Meaningful to the target audience
- Engaging, by use of a strong angle

As you expand your media buys you need to understand the changing demands of customers and find new angles to launch campaigns for different targets.

Support the Prime

There are a variety of ways to bolster the Prime and the angles you develop. Consider each option carefully.

Endorsements and Testimonials

Endorsements and testimonials can be enormously effective. People want to know they are not the only one taking the plunge to buy the product. Moreover, these are freebees in your research because you can easily secure them from the customer service department, online stores, or Amazon reviews of the product.

Pricing

Pricing models are truly an art form. As I've said, often the price of the product is not in the control of the Media Buyer—but how you *present the pricing* is in your power and extremely important. For example, one strategy that is often used is to show the user an obviously expensive full retail price first, then show them the discounted price. Nothing actually changes except for the consumer's expectation: after seeing a high full retail price, the regular price seems reasonable. I can almost hear Ron Popeil, a direct-to-consumer titan, proclaiming what you will *not* pay to buy his famous food dehydrator. "You're not going to spend $129.95 for it! You're not going to spend $120.00, not $115, not even $100! Not $90! Not $80! And not even $70 like you may all be thinking! All you spend for this fabulous machine, and I know you can all afford this, is just four easy payments of $14.99!"[7]

But it doesn't stop there because the announcer interrupts Ron; it turns out the food dehydrator's final cost, plus free slicer gift, is only two easy payments of $19.99.

You want to present the price as a good deal—a *great* deal—and you don't want the price to negatively reflect on quality. Even if something is a high-end product, it can also be a comparatively great deal. Ron Popeil was a master, and much of his advertising legacy is available to watch on YouTube.

"Free" is a powerful word that can almost always gain the attention of your prospective buyer. But the only time you can use it is when something is *actually* free. You absolutely, positively, cannot make deceptive or untruthful promises to secure a sale. Be aware, as well, that on platforms such as Facebook the word "free" may flag your ad and result in it being banned or put into review. A good alternative is "no cost" or something similar.

The Secret

You can specially motivate people by convincing them you have inside information, a secret to share. You're doing them a favor by granting them access to a secret they could never know about, until they found you.

To land sales with your secret knowledge, you must convince the customer that:

- You have information they don't have
- There is a reason and story behind the information
- There's a reason why you're sharing it, or will share it with them
- The information you have is highly valuable
- You could never just give this information away

Secrets are easy to write and can almost be templated. Here are the ingredients to a successful secret angle:

- Set up intrigue intertwined with how the secret is beneficial for the customer
- Hook with a strong headline, and make the rest easy to digest
- Talk in circles around the inside information, and never actually release it

The consumer must become an insider, too, in order for them to know everything you know… And you have to be the best and only person to get them to become one.

Make Real Time Limits, the Sense of Urgency

Time can be a tricky matter from a regulatory perspective. You need and want to create action, but you cannot mislead the consumer with a fabricated or false sense of urgency. A true sense of urgency is worth trying to create because it is a motivator for sales that has been well-documented by psychologists: it works and works well. *Buy this product now! Or you could be too late…*

Again, you must be honest, but you can also be compelling using natural time limits. Consider all of the reasons it may be important for a customer to have the product now rather than later, and all of the reasons they may regret waiting too long to buy. These reasons can tie in with the times and the seasons, for example.

The term for this concept is Fear Of Missing Out (FOMO). Human beings have a strong internal desire to avoid missing out on an opportunity. Users of social media are especially likely to feel FOMO; it's tied into their love of social media itself. FOMO can work very well in a short-buy cycle, but you do need to be careful how you activate it. Try to avoid being overly sensational or making exaggerated claims about the possibility of missing out. This is a tool best used somewhat subtly; time counters, limited free shipping, and expiring content are good examples.

Make it Easy

Make sure the customer can click through to the next page with ease. The pages need to flow like a river. Make it simple to buy lots and make choices. Remember Hick's Law: The time it takes to make a decision increases with the number and complexity of choices.[8]

The take-away from this is, as follows:

- Break components down into smaller steps; remember the narrowing concept of funnels and gain commitment from your buyer in increments, a little at a time

- Highlight the best purchasing option and make clear what most people want, showing for example the most popular items or linking potential purchases

- Use technology to progressively disclose the information

There must be *no impediment to buying*. On the contrary, it should feel like the easiest thing in the world. A natural outcome from reading the ad material.

Social Proof

To understand the value of social proof you need look no further than bartenders, buskers, and baristas who cleverly place a few crisp bills on the tip jar. The visual stimulus functions as a motivator. The result equals more tips.

Social proof works because people will, in an uncertain situation, look to the behavior of others to determine the correct action to take. This is a behavior that is hard-wired into us. If there is an empty jar on the bar, the customer will assume no one else is tipping—the conclusion, they don't need to do it either. But if there is already money in the jar, the customer will believe everyone else is doing it—so they determine they ought to tip as well.

There is, of course a limit: a one-hundred-dollar bill in the jar is unlikely to spur a series of enormous tips. It's not proportional to the situation; it loses its believability as well as its possibility. The key is that people do these things without really thinking about them. If they're prompted to stop and think something to the effect of, "Hey, a hundred dollars is way more than I can afford—who leaves that kind of tip anyway?" then the phenomenon is disrupted and loses its effectiveness.

Social proof has to be subtle. It needs to be information that is easily accepted and not overly questioned. The concept can be further broken down into types, as follows:

Users/Peers/Friends

This is evidence that people have bought and/or used the product and are recounting their real-life experiences. They may or may not be within a user's close circle of friends, but through the convenience of social media the consumer can follow these prior purchasers or see their comments.

Experts/Doctors

These are scientists, doctors, teachers, any number of experts pertaining to a particular field or area related to the product—who endorse purchasing the product. Experts can be formal (as in holding a university degree that makes them an expert) or informal (as in a human being who asserts their own expertise). When these people give their opinions, customers are likely to believe the recommendations because of the expert's credentials or assertions of experience in the field.

Celebrities

Approval or endorsements from celebrities (paid or unpaid) are likely to influence buying behavior and capture the attention of customers. But when the celebrity is clearly being paid to promote the product, the effectiveness of their celebrity endorsement is somewhat diminished. Because the "paid to do it" assumption goes along with traditional celebrity endorsement, the angle can be less effective than others—yet can certainly work in particular situations. Moreover, if the celebrity can be seen *using the product* in a way that *doesn't appear to be advertising*, doubt dissipates, and the effectiveness of the endorsement increases. And there are some ingenious ways to draw on vicarious product placement...

Influencers

An Influencer is a person or group that has the ability to influence the behavior or opinions of others through social media. Sometimes they are experts, sometimes they are entertainers, many times their credibility is entirely based on the quantity of their followers. They occupy a sort of grey area between celebrity and friend. We have tested many ways to support the Prime of a product, and influencers are by far the most interesting angle opportunity; harnessing their power is essential.

In our first attempts to use influencers we treated them as click sources. We hired major influencers with major platforms. By this I mean we would hire a major influencer and buy a post or content from them with the goal of that post producing clicks on our product, which would then lead to a CPA. What we learned was that, by and large, this is not what you are buying when you have an influencer post. You are not buying clicks; you are buying an endorsement of credibility.

Interestingly, when most influencers post a commercial endorsement, they leave the post up for a fixed period of time, then delete it. *Why?* The influencers know their followers are mostly interested in them, their lifestyle, their experiences and expertise, and their amazingly entertaining content. They don't necessarily want to follow an Instagram or TikTok or Facebook feed that is based solely on weight loss tea, or a makeup product, or particular fashion items for sale.

So how do you take advantage of an influencer budget? *Copy their post and repost it before the original gets deleted.* Use the post in developing your sales funnels and e-commerce stores.

Pops-Ups

As a purchase activity is taking place, a buyer may be helped to take the leap if they learn of someone else who is *also currently purchasing the product alongside them.* For example, Mrs. Smith of Arizona just bought *two* of the items in question! Such information might best be delivered via a sudden pop-up that fills their screen.

Testimonials

Place the favorable words of real-life users in conspicuous places. If you don't have any of your own testimonials for a product, secure them from customer service or online reviews.

Best/Top Sellers

Mark the packages and products that sell the best with *Recommended, Best-Seller, Almost Sold Out,* or *Limited Inventory.* People want to buy what's hot, what everyone else wants, and what they *almost* cannot have...

Images/Video

Show the product in use or being used by people who are representative of the target customer. This can be done with stills or video. The concept: People like you are doing it, they need it, they use it... *Why not you?*

Total Sold

We all know the famous *XX Billion Served.* These total-user counts make people not want to be left out on something everyone else is clearly doing. After all, only an excellent restaurant would have served billions of hamburgers, right?

Summing Up

The angle is your way into successfully marketing the product. The angle is determined by your Prime along with the target audience in relation to the product.

Purchases must be easy for the customer to make; there is no wiggle room for error. If it isn't simple to navigate a sale, you lose sales.

Seeing others use a product, testimonials, social proof, and notions of scarcity can also provide you with angles into sales. Deals and secrets make a product that addresses a real-life problem seem that much more desirable. A successful Media Buyer will take good advantage of the psychological and social phenomenon wherein people will copy the actions of others when making choices about their own behavior.

CHAPTER 6:

THE ART OF IMAGERY

I have often debated the importance of copy over art and vice-versa. I have met and trained far more marketing artists than writers in my life, but what does this mean?

The skill of copywriting is far rarer than that of an artist in the world of layout advertisements. And perhaps I am harsher with the wordsmiths than I am with the artists.

I have seen art evolve over the years. Hand sketches, computer drawings, Photoshop. So many young people pick up a laptop, sign up for a graphic design course, and decide they want to be an artist. The best I have worked with are obsessive workaholics who believe in themselves and don't take criticism well. They work to evolve what they do and make high-performing ads.

The worst I have worked with are artists who feel there is an end to the time commitment and an end to the process of marketing. They say things like, "It's good enough, it will work." Coming to a full stop as such doesn't account for the dynamic flow and commitment to success that's essential to media buying.

After many years of not having worked in the health and beauty industry, I was pleased to see knockoffs of the diet and muscle templates that were created by a young artist I trained years ago. These templates were still being sold for a pretty penny. This is a true success story, and it stands the test of time.

Yet the use of images and video is more about knowing when *not* to use them than it is about knowing when to use them. *What does this mean?*

I have trained many young artists and creative people, from print media to online front-end development to video, and one who stands out is someone I met when I first arrived in Vietnam and commenced training a completely new team of artists and front-end developers. An ambitious and successful manager had been building our funnels and pages and he eventually came to me with a proposal.

Basically, he said, "Bruce, our funnels and pages look terrible. They are boring, there is no flavor, no spice, no excitement." He then presented me with a new look and design for a page, which was amazing. It was artistically beautiful. It had sexy models. It had vibrant, full colors and amazing floral borders; it was visually balanced and was certainly worthy of submission for a leading marketing award, or to make the cover of a glossy magazine.

I sat him down and I said we don't win awards. There is no award for high click-through rates, there is no award for conversion rate. And there is no award for making the client money. Then I started to go through each of the elements that were added to this page. I asked him, "Will this fancy border lead to a conversion? Will this fancy font lead to click-through to the checkout? Will this beautiful graphic move the customer through the funnel?" Each time the answer was no, and each time we took that particular item off the page. Soon we were left pretty much where he had begun, which was a very clean, non-distracting page on which every image and graphic had one purpose: to create click-through or conversion. To make sales.

Whoever said that a picture is worth a thousand words was probably someone trying to get out of writing a thousand words. Visuals and words have different functions in advertising and attempting to substitute one for the other is a roadmap to failure.

The images that you select need to meet the basic requirement of relevance, and what is relevant is determined by the copy. Very rarely is an image so powerful that we change the copy to match it. The normal process is for graphic artists to bring the existing copy alive by curating and making images that fit with it. Read the copy and make sure the images and videos match; if they don't, get rid of them.

I have always believed that words must lead the art, not vice-versa. Having said that, in media buying we must convince potential customers to click through from the media they begin with. Depending on whether that media is search or social, the presence of an image or video can be highly important to get them "out of the platform" and into our world.

The word is convincing and provides the push to ensure the buying behavior, but your image choices must be sound and chosen carefully and cautiously.

My first rule of images is to show the potential customer the product in an unobscured way. Remove anything that does not materially contribute to the message of the copy. *But how does one select images to enhance copy to create great advertisements?* One concept I try to drill into all artists I work with is to understand the medium and build to the medium.

I come from the world of paper. As a young lawyer, we had two kinds of paper. There was letter-sized, which was used for all communication, and legal sized, which was used for a variety of legal documents. Both types were eight and a half inches wide, but the letter size was eleven inches long, and although the extra space was never really used, the legal was fourteen inches long. In the bad old days of direct marketing, we went to great lengths to select which parts of the letter or legal would show through the envelope window. This is what would be seen first when receiving the mail, even before opening it. The window acted as a teaser for what could be hidden and revealed on inner pages.

But that was a long time ago, back when I had to fight off velociraptors on my way into work. Today, in the age of computers and the internet, the medium has been turned upside down and we've found ourselves face-to-face with never-before-seen realities. Imperative: You do not want to allow potential customers to click away from your advertisement.

Keeping this necessity in mind, first, we must do whatever we can to keep the potential customer engaged. Possibilities are to give customers images that catch their eye, ask them a question, or suggest an action. But the page is no longer eleven or fourteen inches long. We have come out of the Stone Age and moved into the era of the continuous page. A second reality is that a person will scroll and scroll and scroll forever, rendering the concept of pages meaningless. Much like reading a book page by page to the finish, as we guide a consumer through a click process using multiple screens, as they see multiple pages and are asked to click through, there is mathematical certainty that *some* people will eventually stop. And yet people are more willing to scroll a continuous page to the bottom, just to see what's there.

So, we use that knowledge to our advantage. When I work with artists, I tell them the page that flows downward is like a river. In my mind as I explain the journey down the page, I visualize the classic movie *African Queen* and the perilous voyage down the Nile. At every twist and turn there is a new inexplicable and exciting adventure. All the while, Hepburn bickers with Bogart, but at the end of the river they're married and sail off into the sunset. Much like our customers, happy with their purchase.

The River of Continuous Page

Taking the reader down the river of continuous page is a journey that requires the artist to understand the copy and pair the art with it. The Media Buyer will consider the links between images and copy; how text and art compliment rather than detract from each other; the interest offered by each image; the story behind it; emotion it evokes; possibilities for movement; humanity it espouses; potential contributions of charts and graphs; intellectualism versus the ability to be understood by all; and finally, the contribution of desire.

Consistency

Create images that are consistent with the copy. There must be flow between the two. The images ought to jibe with the copy and must never contradict it (except in rare circumstances where the contradiction is being capitalized on). The images themselves flow in style and consistent design. Images ought to be consistent in their connection with the Prime as well as consistently appropriate for the platform context, the style of advertisement, the price point, and the type of product.

Complimentary

The images should bring the copy to life. They enhance it. For the *African Queen,* would we show a crocodile or a casino? Are there Nazis or a PETA ship saving animals? Think of the possibilities and the meaning created by each, or the further meaning you can achieve when you *combine images*. Remember that the images are there to serve your purpose, which is harmonious with the words and which compliments them. Complimentary images can also create a story or an emotion in their relationship to each other: but again, be sure this serves your purpose and not simply a feeling or narrative in and of itself.

Interest

Does the photo or image do its job? Does it actually create strong interest in the copy and push a reader to read, then ultimately buy? How do you know if it creates that interest? If you don't know, go back a few chapters and refresh yourself on the necessity of solid research. Often images can help a consumer visualize themselves using a product, or they can form a connection between a product and problem. These types of images generate interest in buying.

Story

Bring in images that tell the adventure. These are images that enhance the copy or images that may even evoke a story on their own. But don't dress the product up in the images: let the consumer see it. The story can be created by the copy, and images can help tell it efficiently. Images that accompany the story are ones that connect the consumer to the product through meaningful narrative. This connection leads to the sale.

Emotion

Images can pull on a consumer's heartstrings, but that's only useful if the emotion they create leads the consumer down the river to buy the product. Altruism, for example, is a great positive emotion that can be brought about with an image. And yet, the image itself isn't enough; the marketing needs to link that feeling to an actual purchase of the product. If the product has a function, you will want to associate positive emotions with it. To accomplish this, you show the end result and not the labor. This is the beauty of an image. Bicycles, for example, are pictured at the end of the journey with the stunning mountain view—not with some sweaty guy in spandex struggling up a hill. Kitchen mixer images feature tempting cupcakes with icing and sprinkles and a candle—they don't showcase the messy kitchen, the lumpy batter, or the heavy mixer being heaved back onto the shelf. Think about including images that encourage a desire for instant gratification because that sensibility can lead to sales. Images can also bring up fears but be wary of taking the shock and awe approach (for reasons previously discussed).

Movement

Video can be incredibly useful when applied correctly. It can add a sense of movement and progression and show an action-effect correlation. Consider using short animated pictures (GIFs) to add some punch to your marketing. GIFs stand out in social feeds and people tend to feel drawn to them because they're fun.

GIFs also can take advantage of the brain's scientifically proven ability to quickly process images, which isn't to say that the GIFs or video should take the place of good copy. They shouldn't. But they might entice a person to notice the copy and then read on. This is their purpose.

Humanity

Be human and use human images. I have certain rules about this and have proven them, but you can prove them to yourself. Don't distort human faces, don't cut them off, and don't obscure them. Use their emotion, their stare, even where they look to create the flow of the continuous page.

Drawings and Charts

I love charts, drawings, and graphs. But if you use them, make them understandable to a six-year-old. Your target audience is not some elite math professor you've never met. If a chart or graph can't be understood by a six-year-old, *it's too complicated.* This is not because the audience is stupid; it's because they're skimming, they're busy, they're doing other things, and you are trying to quickly and efficiently steal them away from that. Capture their attention with something pretty and make the pertinent information digestible in mere seconds of attention.

Intellectual

Don't do it. *Just do not do it.* Look at it, then toss it away. If it has even a sprinkling of being "intellectual" it will fail. No one cares. Pictures take up space. Space spent on intellectual mumbo-jumbo is wasted space. Keep your eye on the prize.

The Average Person, or Less

Always assume that you are speaking to the most everyday person you can imagine buying or using the product. If there is humor, or anything that requires additional thought, that humor and thought must be apparent to all, even the most oblivious dullard.

Desire

Yes, sex sells, but use it sparingly and only when appropriate. The suggestion of sex can grab someone's attention but, depending on who the audience is, sex could also easily repel them. Consider that once a person is thinking about sex it is difficult to get them to think about the product you're trying to sell, unless they can directly assume it will help them obtain sex.

Ultimately

The world of imagery that is available to us for marketing is vast and can prove exciting. Artists seem to be plentiful, but perhaps the best ones are few and far between. It is important, however, to *never substitute an image for the right words*.

The notion that pictures should take the place of a slogan or headline is false. Rather, the images you use in your marketing are meant to enhance the copy. And they are meant to convey the Prime.

User Generated Content (UGC) tends to convert best because these days most social media users are incredibly jaded about ads. They can spot a heavily branded ad in their feed easily and are conditioned to skip over it. However, if you can make your ad appear—even for just a split second—to be content they believe was shared by a friend or family member, you have a much higher chance of success.

Images are specifically chosen, designed, and placed to compliment the words or story told in the advertisement—to assist the copy in doing its job, which is the job of making sales. Images will flow as the copy flows, and the river leads to the final purchase. If it doesn't do that, you're doing it wrong.

CHAPTER 7:

THE WONDER OF WORDS

Judith Charles' classic quote, "A copywriter is a sales-person behind a typewriter," offers the opening line to Robert Bly's seminal work on copywriting.[9] While you are hopefully not using a typewriter to create copy for online media buying, the sentiment remains true.

You may be entertaining, but you are not an entertainer. You may be funny, but you are not a comedian. You may be smart, but you are not a professor. You are a writer of advertising and if your words don't lead to sales you are a failure.

Let's accept it. Copy rules. You must either write it yourself or be blessed with the gift of being able to differentiate copy that sells from copy that flops. Good Media Buyers can identify bad copy and bask in the beauty of amazing compelling copy. Milton Glaser would have been an amazing Media Buyer, and oftentimes graphic designers do make great Media Buyers because design is so integral to grabbing attention. But Glaser also had a brilliant obsession with words meeting imagery. In his Ted Talk in 1998 he relayed a story of driving in the countryside with his wife and seeing a sign. Glaser commented to his wife, something to the effect of, "That is a fabulous piece of design." The sign he saw read:

RELIABLE DUTCHMEN
AUTO REPAIR

In the Ted Talk, Glaser explained, "Well, it's so persuasive, because the purpose of that sign is to get you into the garage, and since most people are so suspicious of garages, and know that they're going to be ripped off, they use the word *reliable*. But everybody says they're reliable. But reliable Dutchman—fantastic!"[10]

Glaser explains that as soon as you hear the word Dutchman—an archaic term because nobody calls Dutch people "Dutchmen" anymore—you get this image of the kid with his finger in the dike preventing it from collapsing and flooding Holland. As a result, the entire issue of shady mechanics gets detoxified by the use of that one word, "Dutchman." Milton goes on to say that if you think he's exaggerating, all you'd have to do is substitute another word, such as Indonesian... Or French. He quips, "Now, 'Swiss' works, but you know it's going to cost a lot of money."

Like Glaser, good Media Buyers are the type in the grocery shop to read all of the copy that sells the condiments, vegetables, and soda. To the chagrin of my family, I often lag behind them reading packages and all the many ads placed in the grocery store. I remember one time being berated by my daughter in the veggie section as I extolled the genius of a brilliant copywriter who put up this sign on the carrots: "Snowman Noses: 25 cents."

She told me it was so uncool; it should refer to them as Snowpersons—as I slipped a bag of noses into our cart. Good Media Buyers seem to have a way of twisting and reinventing words to shed new light on the product through powerful angles. And of course, the best, the elite, put their ideas to the A/B test until they find something that is proven to shine.

Over the years I've always enjoyed the cooperation and collaboration I've had with great writers. As CEO of DFO Global it is not really my job to do the copywriting, but many times I see it cross my desk, particularly as new brands are built. I view much of the copy that we create and certainly still have time to read and review headlines. Copywriters are perhaps the unsung heroes of direct marketing; however, I see posts on Facebook chats such as, "Anyone have a cheap copywriter for a few paragraphs?" It was the great David Ogilvy who once reminded us, "Pay peanuts, says Jimmy Goldsmith, and you get monkeys."[11] I've always kept great copywriters on retainer: great copywriters offer a creative voice that leads to inspiring products and brand angles.

When thinking about copy there are certain basic characteristics that lend themselves to media buying. These are the ones that stick out to me. Copywriters for media buying tend to:

- Naturally write in second person
- Write short in headlines and long in body
- Know which words need to be highlighted, instinctively
- Work the angles—all of them
- Naturally use power words where appropriate, such as "Act Now" or "Free Today"
- Build more than one option and never stop testing
- Ask questions and dig in
- Ideas, ideas, ideas! Flow to excess, solve decisively, then move on to the next great idea

The first step in editing great copy is to cut out all the content that is obviously unusable. Lay it aside, forget about it, don't even try if:

- It is offensive or violates sound principles
- It is not relevant to the product
- It is not yours, or the permissions to use it aren't in place

Now we are left with the remaining copy, which you either made or has been made available to you. Let's learn how to decide exactly what to select.

Here are some considerations:

- Bring forward all of the copy that speaks to you as a human being
- Bring forward the copy that elicits some emotional reaction
- Eliminate the long, boring, and verbose from your headlines
- Eliminate or change complex words to simple direct language
- If needed, enlist that six-year-old who should also be viewing your graphs
- Select from the above anything written in everyday conversational language

Now that you have your copy to work with, I'll show you that buying media means selecting the *best* copy or making it yourself. Media Buyers are natural writers or naturally good at borrowing what is great writing.

The headline is the first piece of copy the customer sees. It is also the most important so it's imperative to lead with your sharpest, most concise copy. This is the hook, the draw, and the essence. Your headline will convey your Prime.

Always remember the hierarchy: headlines dominate the sub headlines and all body copy. Spend your time on what matters: headlines.

Why Headlines Are Important

There are a few reasons why headlines dominate over other types of copy. First, people will not invest themselves in the rest of the content unless the first thing they read really engages them. Engage the reader and you have won their interest. Otherwise, you've lost them at hello.

Second, if the headline is convincing and engaging, the copy that follows is colored by that headline. The user will effectively interpret the rest of the copy in this guided manner and will be more receptive to what you are selling them. Think of a headline as a lens that focuses everything the user will subsequently read. You have the power to shape their thinking in this way.

Moreover, once people make up their mind, they start to skim through the body copy. Instead of spending equal time on body copy and headlines, people digest the headline, use that as a summary, and breeze over the rest.

Most people want things to be easy and if you deliver them convincing hooks, you've done your job in the headline. Just don't lose them with the body copy by being:

- Stupid
- Offensive
- Illogical
- Inconsistent
- Boring
- Wordy
- Overly sensational

With a great headline and sufficiently supporting body text, you've arrived at the number one purpose of good direct marketing copy, which is to motivate the reader to take action. The surest way to do this is to appeal to their needs and desires in a clear and logical way—so they can see that what's being offered can satisfy them at an emotional level.

There is a well-known metric that says you have "three seconds to stop the scroll." Users spend about three seconds or fewer on an image or ad in their newsfeed before scrolling on. Within those three seconds, you have to capture their attention.

Some of my favorite ad headlines:

- I've Fallen and Can't Get Up!
- Protected by More Prenups Than Any Other Car
- They Don't Write Songs About Volvo
- To All Those Who Use Our Competitors' Products, Happy Father's Day

Another favorite is the "Reliable Dutchman Auto Repair!" admired by Milton Glaser. Amazing! Appeal to consumer emotions by capturing the combination of frugality and reliability associated with the Dutch. It's simple and effective. It's catchy, and it works.

People are bombarded with headlines. Imagine you are an explorer on an icefield in Antarctica. Ahead of you are hundreds of thousands of penguins, all squawking at you. They all desperately want you to listen to them and only them. That is how your consumer feels when browsing online...

You, the copywriter, are a penguin. Your squawk is your headline.

Above all else, your headline needs to grab the potential customer's attention. Somehow you need to stand out from the rest. To do this, you have to appeal to them. You want to offer them something they want, help them solve a problem, and you need to do it so efficiently it fits in a mouthful of words. Appeal to the consumer's self-interest. Avoid gimmicks—a naked body might get you the attention you want, but it's a distraction more than anything. Ask yourself, how is this going to lead to a sale?

Highly likely your consumer who's interested in clicking on a nude photo will go off in another direction when the checkout shows up—specifically, they'll veer off in the direction of other naked photos. Unless the product you are selling directly relates to that.

If you succeed in getting your customer's attention, your headline can serve as a sort of triage system selecting the attention of the customers for whom your product is likely to appeal and weeding out those whom it isn't. If you're selling a self-cleaning cat litter box, for example, you don't really need or want the attention of people who are not cat owners. You want to attract the people who have and love their cats.

Your ad can also deliver your message to the high percentage of people who don't bother to read any of the rest of your copy—ad guru David Ogilvy suggests that four out of five people will only look at the headline and skip the rest of the ad.[12] Either the headline convinces them to buy, or they will not be convinced. It is always a good idea to work the product's name into the headline for this reason. Remember our discussion of falloff...

For those who will take the time to examine your whole ad, the headline is what draws them in, which is particularly important to consider for products that require you to educate the consumer or explain in greater detail why they want to purchase it. If your target requires information to convince them to make the purchase, your headline should pull them *into* the ad so that they can receive this information.

There are a number of different types of headlines worth individual discussion.

Direct Headlines

Which are exactly as they sound like. It's all in the headline. "Brand Name Eyeglasses at one-tenth of the price!" Not all products lend themselves to these sorts of headlines, but when they do, use them.

Indirect Headline

These attract attention and arouse curiosity. They are good for when you need to draw the reader into the body of the ad. A great example of an indirect headline is "Melts in your mouth, not in your hands." What does? Why? One will have to read to see.

Instructional Headline

Such as, "Remove your wrinkles in three easy steps." Key to these is that the promised instructions are clear and simple. If it seems like it will be difficult, people will not click through. "Remove your wrinkles eventually after many tricky steps that I will now explain to you" would obviously be the opposite of what's called for here.

News Headline

Are headlines that mimic a headline from a news source. They engage curiosity and are usually followed by an ad that also resembles a news source. These headlines will draw a reader into an advertorial, for example.

Command Headline

As the name suggests, is a headline which essentially orders the reader to do something. The most famous of these is Nike's "Just do it."

Question Headline

Asks a question, usually either a leading one, or one that is provocative, or both. "What's in your wallet?" "Can you hear me now?"

Reason Why Headline

Also known as begging the question. L'Oréal: "Because you're worth it." This is a good one that appeals to a sense of self-worth.

Testimonial

Such as, "Recommended by four out of five dentists." Who are these five dentists? No one knows. No one cares. If four out of five of them are recommending you chew Trident, who are you to argue with that?

Benefit

Greyhound's "Leave the driving to us" is a great example of finding the golden ticket. Riding the bus doesn't have a whole lot of benefits. It tends to smell bad, take a long time, and give you motion sickness. But Greyhound zeroed in on the main, good thing, and made it their headline. That is of course, also the Prime.

The Characteristics of Good Copy

Good copy sits in the reader's mind and swims amongst their emotions. If the spirit moves them and the logic plays out, they will buy. Ask yourself: Do I want to use this product after reading that? Does it make me dream of the product and desire it in my life?

Only good copy and good headlines make you feel like your life would improve instantly if you could wave a magic wand and have that product right next to you. That is consumer gratification, and media buying leans heavily on this.

Next, there are some essential considerations—such as knowing your goals and remaining focused on your Prime—and you will want to take each into account in your creation of good copy.

Remain focused on the Prime

It's called the Prime for a reason. Everything you are doing is about delivering this message. It is easy to get distracted by your own words, ideas, jokes, whatever. Highlight your product's benefits, know your competition's weaknesses. While it's not a great idea to attack or even directly reference your competition, you need to be aware of what makes your product better or different from theirs. You want your copy to highlight these attributes as clearly and succinctly as possible, without inadvertently sending your buyer off to look at something else.

Know your Goals

Your words exist to create an action. What is that action? Is it to get a click-through? Is it to get an add-on sale? Whatever it is, focus on that outcome.

Address the Customer

Don't talk about the company, or the brand, as a "we." Don't say "We can deliver you this blender." Instead, talk about the customer. The customer is the focus, and the ad is all about satisfying them. "You can be blending like this by tomorrow…"

Use the Active Voice

In the active voice, you have a subject and an active verb, which is often a person and a specific action related to the project. "You will clean floors effortlessly!" In the passive voice, the subject is the recipient of the action. This means something is acted upon, which tends to be a wordier way of saying it, and less exciting. Compare: "Your floors will be effortlessly cleaned by you." This difference may not seem like a big deal, but you want people to *envision themselves taking action*. This is their connection to the product. You want them to act, not be acted upon.

Evaluate Your Copy

Entrepreneur Michael Masterson developed a useful tool for evaluating the effectiveness of copy (it is commonly applied to headlines but works well for copy as a whole). While there are obviously some exceptions to his approach, it offers a pretty decent starting point as outlined by Robert W. Bly in his *The Copywriter's Handbook*, specifically: "The Four U's of copywriting: Unique, Urgent, Ultra-Specific and Useful."[13]

Here is more about each "U" in detail:

- **Unique**. Your copy should make it clear what differentiates your product from all the others. Also, what differentiates the buyer for buying it... If the product is something more generic, you can still find a way to say something new and unique about it.

- **Urgent**. Nobody wants to miss out on an opportunity. If your copy doesn't present an element of timeliness, there is less of a reason for the customer to buy at that moment. You want them to make that decision, and you want them to make it now. Urgency can be created in a number of ways using deadlines, product scarcity, a deal that will expire, or even the end of the current season or an upcoming holiday.

- **Ultra-Specific**. This one is stretching the "U" convention, but basically what it means is that the copy should be completely focused on the attributes and benefits of the product or service. No filler, no distractions. This is also about honing your words, choosing the most effective diction, and making every word and image count. You have only so much space, and only so much of your busy target consumer's time.

- **Useful**. The copy should communicate how the product will not just be of use, but how it will improve the life of the customer. The product you sell will make them happier, solve a problem, fulfill a desire, and so forth. No one wants to buy useless items. Tell the customer how the product will be of use to them (as opposed as how to use it), and they will be far more receptive. Get them to *imagine* themselves using the product... Even better, try to get them to the point where they can't imagine living without it!

The idea behind Masterson's "4 U's" tool as discussed by Bly is that you can use it to evaluate your copy and assign it a score from one to four, based on each of the criteria. You won't often score a perfect four, and your actual score is irrelevant, but if you take a look and score low in more than one of these areas, you probably need to re-examine your copy. Use the tool to help you refine your work.

Overall

Keep your sentences short and active. Keep your paragraphs tight and focused. Stay committed to the creation of action. Stay focused on the product. Say what you need to say clearly, simply, and accurately. Be committed to making the sale.

I'll leave you with the words of the great Mark Twain: "Don't use a five-dollar word when a fifty-cent word will do." Twain wasn't a copywriter, but if he was, I'd have hired him.

CHAPTER 8:

TRACKING AND BUYING

Jesse James probably doesn't know the science behind his arc welder, but he sure knows that it works and what to do with it. He put it to good use fabricating the El Diablo 2000 Camel Roadhouse Bike.

Basically, you can wield tools that have great power and produce a beautiful result without ever knowing how they do what they do—so long as you know what they're good for and when to put them into action. You need to be sure that they *do* work, as well as when they'll work, and when they'll fail.

Tracking Media

Tracking is one of the key tools for the Media Buyer and also the most daunting. If you accept my proposition that all you need to know is that tracking works, that it is necessary and reliable, then skip the next few paragraphs. Otherwise, here is a basic explanation of how and why we track our advertisements and their performance.

I have to use the word *cookie* because it is the truly classic method of tracking online traffic. Here's how cookies work: Whenever your computer visits a webpage, it talks to the server that sends you the webpage. During that interaction your computer sends out a packet of information we call the browser fingerprint, and the website you visit places a small packet of code in your browser: this is called a cookie.

Cookies are powerful. They are code and they have function, including reading and writing content on your computer. It's likely that cookies will become irrelevant in a few years as we shift to Conversions API, but the basic concept will remain the same.

Tracking software works by *placing a label in your cookies*. When you load the page there will be code and image files that fire in the event of you loading the page to the software. Presto, you have been tracked.

Tracking is also done using *tracking pixels*. A tracking pixel is basically an HTML code snippet, which is loaded when a user visits a website or views an email.

It fires when your computer loads it and reports your activity to the owner of the tracking pixel.

The tracking pixel is used by advertisers and their media providers, such as Google and Facebook, to acquire data for online marketing and analysis. It can also be used to locate you on later sites for effective *retargeting*.

When we know where a customer came from, and when they visit more pages, we can identify them.

Big companies like Google and Facebook share this tracking information between them. The classic method for tracking customers is by cookie, but the browser packet your browser necessarily sent to the webpage can also be used to track you.

Your browser identity, although not always completely unique, is distinct enough that when combined with some basic machine learning, we can tell if it is you.

In the world of performance marketing, affiliates and media buying, how does the tracking get put in place?

Tracking is important in the media buying world because without it, you are guaranteed to burn money. Imagine spending $100,000 a day on campaigns only to learn that you didn't record a single sale. You wouldn't be able to identify if your ads yielded any sales, let alone know which ads your customers bought from. And these are such major benefits to online advertising: accurate information we could only strive for and waste time attempting to gather back in the days of only print.

In addition, the biggest ad platforms typically have an algorithm that combines tracking and Artificial Intelligence (AI) in order to optimize for specific marketing goals.

For example, suppose I'm running a Facebook campaign to generate more purchases. The more purchases I record to FB, the better the FB algorithm can start to identify its users with the highest probability of making a purchase from me—while also eliminating the ones who likely won't. This kind of information saves a Media Buyer both time and money.

There is much tracking software available for media buying, and it's basically plug-and-play. Google provides a service called Google Tag Manager (GTM). GTM is a tag management system used to load HTML, CSS, and JavaScript code on webpages, typically for tracking purposes. Essentially it is a piece of JavaScript code placed in the header of a webpage that often serves as a container for tracking pixels.

Basically, GTM gives a Media Buyer the ability to control and place multiple tracking pixels on any of these pages, while being relatively easy to use. When the software is used correctly, marketers can track almost any type of interaction on a webpage. The data tracked can then be used to optimize campaigns and obtain a deeper understanding of how users interact with your website. Marketers who are able to analyze this data will have more opportunities to improve their marketing campaigns.

But when does the tracking break down, what is the Achilles heel, the kryptonite to tracking?

I am sitting here and thinking about tracking. Is there a funny story to tell? Is there an anecdote to bring home tracking and the issues that go along with it? Well, this is about as funny as it gets. So, this guy starts a campaign, and the tracking is perfect. He increases spend on Friday night and checks the campaign Monday and discovers the tracking code has fallen off and his entire spend did not convert... I guess that's not so funny. Another one... How many Media Buyers does it take to get great tracking? Answer: It takes only one small error to throw off the tracking and ruin the campaign and spend. *Hmm.* That's not funny either. How about a story about how Mac computers can cut off certain characters when copying and pasting, and then your tracking pixel is not fully placed? Are you laughing yet?

When tracking is done *right* you get paid and you laugh all the way to the bank as your sources give you better and better traffic. There are only sad and embarrassing stories to tell when tracking failed, and in-between stories when it partially failed and caused people to give up on a campaign that could have been successful. Let's not go down that path of failure.

Tracking fails for a number of reasons, some that make common sense and some that are more technical. First, people frequently change devices, and in these instances, you lose the cookie and the browser fingerprint. People also change their browsers when the "same result" cookie is not in use, or they go incognito and tracking is hampered but not always defeated.

In addition, there are a host of technical issues that can surface, mostly related to device connection and tracking set up. Some cookies fail to load due to issues related to internet service disruption.

More common is failure of the code that writes the cookie. Sometimes too many requests are made, and they simply do not all make it through. To avoid this problem, GTM recommends using a maximum of six tags on a page.

Buying Media

There are three main sources of media for you to purchase, and each has its own idiosyncrasies. Your sources are as follows:

- Search Engine
- Social Media
- Native Traffic

Let's take a look at each in more detail.

Figure 4. Traffic sources.

Search Engine Traffic

Tapping into or generating search engine traffic that will view your ad, click through to checkout, and ultimately buy your product, is of importance to any Media Buyer. Search engines play a major, apparent role in directing online customers to your product.

The basic concept is this: Media Buyers can bid on keywords that the users of services such as Google and Yahoo might enter when looking for certain products or services. The keywords give the Media Buyer the opportunity for their ads to appear alongside results for those search queries.

The top search engines of interest to you are:
- Google
- YouTube
- Amazon
- Facebook

- Bing
- Baidu
- Yandex

Google is by far the most influential and most powerful. It dominates online advertising. You can be certified by Google to buy from Google, and you'd be foolish to not self-certify.

The process is simple and completed in three easy steps:

- Register for a Google partner account
- Pass the Google ads fundamentals test with 80%
- Pass the Google ads exam, again with 80% or higher

Media Buyers who don't take advantage of this are selling themselves short. But how does *search traffic* work?

Really it is so simple you don't even need to do the tests (except really you do). Search traffic is when a user types a keyword or a phrase into a search engine and clicks a result in order to access their desired content—then, for example, Google places an ad above it.

All you need to know is which keywords will work with the product you are selling. Again, to do this correctly you need to know your product. Also, you need to do your research and have a basic understanding of possible searches. You can even buy the brand names of competitors or similar products as keywords that can direct those searches to your pages!

Paid search is when a Media Buyer purchases the ad space that is sold by a search engine in relation to the keyword or phrase that a user submits. Paid searches put your ad to the top of the list and can be effective in generating clicks.

Display Traffic

Display traffic is ad space on a website that is for sale typically on a Cost Per Mille (CPM) basis. The cost of the advertising is based on how many thousand impressions are provided. This ad space can be a banner, text link, or native content within an article.

But this is probably not where a beginner starts.

Social Media

A *social network* is an online network that people use to engage with their friends or family, or even to meet new people. The goal is to connect users who have similar interests, activities, and lifestyles; thus, perhaps, similar tastes in products we can sell.

Social network media buying focuses on social networking services where advertisements are shown to users based on information gathered from target group profiles. Social networks can vary in format but share this similar feature of interest to Media Buyers: highly targeted traffic at inexpensive prices.

The top social networks are:

- Facebook
- Twitter
- LinkedIn
- Instagram
- Snapchat
- Pinterest
- Reddit

Paid social media ads are very powerful. Perhaps more than ever before because social media can target particular demographics to the Media Buyer's benefit. The information and knowledge only grow with time.

Social media knows age ranges, it knows your education level, and it knows who owns a home... Ads can target specific areas, localize based on zip codes or mile radiuses, and even go after certain job titles.

If you think elementary school teachers might especially want to buy the page of gold star stickers you're marketing for their students, well, you can have that. And your teachers become a bajillion times more likely to see that ad than a carpenter... Moreover, thanks to tracking, you won't have to make up a number like bajillion; you can learn the precise number of times your teachers see your ad and interact.

Facebook also certifies you for buying ads. Facebook Blueprint offers step-by-step instructions on how to buy Facebook advertisements. This is also something you should do.

In short: I would not work with a junior Media Buyer unless they had the Google and Facebook certifications.

Native Traffic

Native traffic is ad space built in and around the content of a website. This type of advertising involves paid ads that match the look, feel, and function of the media in which they appear.

Native marketing can take the form of an ad that is informational or an ad that closely resembles the content of the webpage where it originates. These ads can appear in your social media newsfeed, wedged between items, hardly recognizable as ads. They can be promoted at the top of a list generated by your favorite search engine. They can be seen as content recommendations that follow an article you just read, especially if you gave it a thumbs up or five stars. They can be hyperlinks embedded in articles… They can be thought of as *ads in disguise*.

Advertorials are another great example, and Media Buyers use these to their advantage. The advertorial takes on properties of an editorial, so initially it may not read as an ad. And yet, it will prompt consumers to buy your product.

Top native networks, use any of the following to gain native traffic:

- Taboola
- Outbrain
- Yahoo Gemini

In short, sourcing great native traffic is indispensable to media buying.

Putting it All Together

Tracking and buying are linked concepts because a savvy Media Buyer will want to track information about ads in order to make the best possible decisions on where and how to buy.

Tracking is how you will find the most advantageous placements for the lowest prices. When buying media, the goal is to find the best place and the right time, the best context, and the most targeted traffic—people who actually click through to sales.

Ultimately tracking, much like the A/B testing I've recommended, will help you find your customers—moreover, your best customers, the ones who return and return. Your media buying choices should reflect careful research and consideration. An asset is of course worthless if the right people never even see it.

CHAPTER 9:

WHERE DOES THE TRAFFIC GO?

Okay, so you've got yourself some media and you've got yourself some traffic. Unless you are trying to recreate a Los Angeles freeway at four o'clock on a Friday afternoon, you need somewhere for that traffic to go.

Let's look at the places you will send your traffic on route to arrival at its ultimate destination: the sale.

There are various paths to send the traffic you buy for e-commerce. The first is the web property. The classic example of web property is Amazon and its e-commerce platform. You can either list your product for sale on Amazon, or drive traffic to somewhere else that has the product listed; however, in this case, the sales experience and upsells are totally controlled by Amazon. And the value of your buy is reduced by a transfer of value to Amazon. For the Media Buyer, this is not a particularly good traffic destination.

Second, is the classic storefront, which is exemplified by a site like Shopify, and also supported by Magento and companies like Big Commerce. Here you set up your own online store using their software and drive traffic to your store.

The problem with this option is that it completely ignores the reality of media buying! You can target your buys using so many factors—so why would you send traffic to a store when you can send it to a specific path designed for that traffic? A store by its nature is a general experience that displays a variety of your products. It is the antithesis of specificity. For this reason, it tends to be a very inefficient and ineffective use of media buying dollars.

The third method is to create online sales funnels. We talked a little about funnels in a previous chapter, and now we're going to really dig into them.

Funnels are used by smart Media Buyers to build a targeted and controlled experience for a product or series of products. They have very limited options to buy and very few (if any) distractions from purchasing.

The funnel narrows and focuses the traffic on the job at hand: buying your product.

An ideal funnel answers all necessary questions and leads the targeted customer to the conclusion that they absolutely need this product. Funnels turn targeted visitors into buyers by curating the experience to the known characteristics of the traffic.

Generally, online sales funnels have a few unique attributes that help push customers along the path to purchase. These attributes include:

- The ability to quickly demonstrate the benefits of the product, brand, or service
- Engaging content that resonates with consumers and entices them further down the funnel
- A flow that minimizes other distractions and pulls the traffic back to the funnel
- The efficient closing of the main sale and an opportunity to buy a complimentary product
- A frictionless checkout experience

It is important for a Media Buyer be able to recognize the properties of a high-performing e-commerce sales funnel.

How to Identify a High-Performing Sales Funnel

E-commerce sales funnels come in all shapes and sizes. I'm going to describe the e-commerce sales funnel for you and outline components the funnels may share, but remember that markets change, times change, and the pieces that make a successful funnel can change.

E-COMMERCE FUNNEL

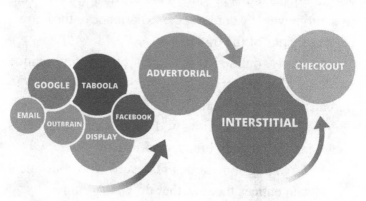

Figure 5. A high-performing e-commerce sales funnel.

Most funnels comprise six important pieces: the advertisement; the presale or advertorial; the interstitial; the checkout or descriptive checkout; the upsell; and confirmation.

The Advertisement

Static and video ads are purchased on platforms where people search for information and view content. These ads are used to engage with targeted consumers; they're designed to push that specific traffic through to the point of sale, not just further a branded message or brand awareness. Much emphasis is placed on headlines that hook the consumer, causing them to click on the ad.

Presale/Advertorial

After clicking on an advertisement, consumers land on sales content, which educates them on the product or brand's value proposition. This is where your Prime is articulated and where the product is framed to your customer. The presale does the work that a brand would normally do. Here is where you may place your advertorial or the like. The consumer is then enticed to click a call-to-action, furthering the sales process.

Interstitial

Often an optional page or pop-up where you summarize the product's characteristics. Customer reviews and testimonials are useful for interstitials. Policies for returns and refund policies can be found here.

Checkout/Descriptive Checkout

Consumers are targeted again with direct response marketing and messaging, which optimizes the funnel and improves the checkout experience. At the bottom of the page, consumers enter their payment information. Once the sale is complete your job is… not yet done!

Upsell

Here consumers are targeted with additional products or services that increase Average Order Value (AOV) and thus widen the gap between customer acquisition cost and value. There's no better time to encourage the purchase of additional products than at the point-of-sale. The credit card number is going in and you know the product your customer wants—now recommend a volume purchase, or a complimentary item they should buy.

Confirmation

Consumers are met with a confirmation message regardless of upsell purchase. It's here that remarketing efforts begin to ensure consumers stay engaged with the brand or suite of products. Email targeting can grow from confirmation. At a high-level, this combination is a great way to maximize a customer's order value and increase customer action (conversion rates), which are both crucial parts of online media buying.

Next, let's dive into the concepts.

Maximizing Order Value

The ultimate marketing goal for a business is to acquire customers at a lower price than the value they provide. Since the acquisition process costs money, the business should strive to optimize the return on that spend wherever possible.

To illustrate this process, think about your last trip to a big box retail store or grocery store. More likely than not, the store had large, bulk item "deals" displayed at the entry point. There may have been signs, "Case Lot Sale!" The store may have offered many small items next to a line of shopping carts or convenience baskets and as you were herded through aisles, you were driven to look at these items.

None of this is by chance, of course. Research data has informed the store that if a customer picks up a cart or a basket, they are likely to buy more. And those products that are super easy to reach and always right in your sight line? Nothing, nothing at all is happening by accident. Everything you see in the store is tailored to your shopping experience, ultimately to upping your purchase.

Now, keep thinking about that same trip. Remember waiting to checkout?

You were probably surrounded by great add-to-cart options. Thirsty? Sports drinks and sodas were on display in a cooler. Out of gum? There were twenty different kinds on the easy-to-reach shelves by the register. If you had a small child with you, they were probably tossing the gum and candy bars in your cart. And those magazines, you may have started reading one then you had to buy it or put it down. You didn't want to put it down. Did it begin to rain outside while you were in there? No problem, I bet you saw the umbrellas for sale halfway down the line, it's that convenient pretty much every time.

The point is that these are all examples of how brick and mortar stores are *designed* to maximize a customer's order value—to get customers into the building to buy what they're looking for and, while they're there, entice them to buy so much more.

These same principles are used to help *maximize order values in online sales funnels.*

Offer customers a great product, then just before they pay, deliver an upsell experience offering a bigger discount when multiple units of the product are purchased. Offer complementary products and services that sit adjacent to the product you're trying to sell. How about the place for some social proof? Here's what everyone else is buying alongside your chosen product. *C'mon, you should do it too...*

The take-away: Even converting a small percentage of customers in this way makes a difference to your media buying success. Remember, though, that this is something you do *once your customer is at the checkout phase*. If you launch into it too early, you create a distraction, which leads to indecision. And you run the real risk of losing your main sale.

Increasing Customer Action (Conversion Rates)

If you've ever shopped on Amazon, and who hasn't, you know how a simple search query turns up dozens of pages of different products, none of which stand out or are particularly enticing. There's no sense of urgency and very little compelling content. Which product should you buy? Should you buy at all?

These are distractions. And Amazon and other branded sites are full of them.

Luckily, sales funnels have a unique ability to limit distractions. They are designed to be streamlined: there are fewer things (and sometimes nothing else) to click. With less to click, it's more likely for customers to stay on the journey you've started them on.

You're making it *easy* for that customer to make a purchase. There's little to do and only one decision to make: to buy, or not to buy. That is the question.

It is absolutely critical that you take into account what sort of device is being used to view your ad. This is a fast-changing issue, and we won't deep dive into it here, but as a general trend: more and more content is viewed on mobile devices and the demands of mobile versus desktop viewing must be taken into account. These are two different beasts.

Other factors that help optimize conversion rate include the following:

- **Multivariate testing.** This is half art and half science. Media Buyers need to know things such as what color call-to-action button works best? Which headline or image has the best purchase rate? Who would actually want to buy a lawnmower? Multivariate testing researches more than one component of a website at a time in a live environment. It can be thought of in simple terms as numerous A/B tests performed on one page simultaneously.

- **Personalization.** How can you better personalize your website to cater to your audience? What shopping experience will cause your traffic to buy?

- **Clarity.** Are you clearly communicating what you want to say? Is it simple? Does your content make sense? Are the images too big or too small? Are they the right image? Are you informing your potential customers, or distracting them, or boring them?

- **Speed.** Does your site load quickly? No one, absolutely no one, wants to wait around to buy. This is probably the single most underrated element of conversion rates. We have seen rates increase from 30% to 70% just by loading the page faster. DFO Global's technology and development division is dedicated to the speed of front-end loads and the speed of banking transactions. *Faster means more sales.*

Increasing customer action is essential, and it happens with the correct set-up and support.

The Backend

The backend includes your customer service and support team, banking and payments, localization, and remarketing and retargeting efforts. Each component of the backend is important to consider.

Customer Service and Support

The customers of a traffic source are the customers of the advertiser—and these become your customers and assets if you capture their contact details. Everyone in contact with your customers should care and take care of them. Customer service on the backend of the offer is therefore an important aspect of selecting an offer. Having great customer service is an absolute necessity in today's world; it's key to conversion rates, and later bringing your customers back for more.

Customer service contributes to the conversion of an offer whether it is in e-commerce or lead generation. It does this because if a customer has questions or concerns about the offer, they are highly likely to abandon the funnel if they cannot reach someone quickly. The more the advertiser can keep the customer *in* the funnel and registering, the higher the conversion rate and the more you will be paid.

Banking and Payments

A very large part of what defines an offer as an e-commerce sales offer is the banking and the approval rates for processing. Some understanding of banking and how it works is valuable in allowing you to assess how well an offer will convert.

Online advertisers have some decisions to make about payments. Imagine, for example, an advertiser's decision to only accept Bitcoin for payment. An exclusive payment method means only customers with access to it—in this case, access to Bitcoin—are able to make the purchase. It follows that the more payment methods you offer, the more potential customers you can accept payments from. That said, you also need to think about the target demographic, who they are and what payment methods they would have. The aim is to secure all payment methods *most commonly used by that demographic*.

For most markets in the United States, it's relatively clear what is needed. Visa and Mastercard are dominant. If you add in Amex and Discover cards you include a large portion of online consumers. On top of that add some wallet payments and PayPal and you are well served.

But if you take that same approach to Germany, for example, it will not be as successful. Germans have some local payment providers, such as Sofort, which are prevalent. In such markets, adding the localized payment options will increase approval rates.

To quickly and easily review any offer and its banking, go to the checkout page and visually check what they accept.

Localization

The concept of translation across international markets has been abandoned in marketing for years. Most performance marketers working globally think instead of the concept of localization, which is creating the look and feel of the online property so that it resembles a local business. The graphics, language, style, and look of the pages should be built to the standard and style of the local market. Simply translating the page into another language does not, and never has, cut it in marketing; try to speak directly to the people in a defined community and area.

The traffic sources also use localization, and their legal compliance is based on the community standards of where the traffic is coming from. *How can you make use of this?*

The best method for avoiding errors of translation is to ask people from the area of interest to review your entire offer. To give you an extreme example of error: I was part of a marketing campaign with which everyone received a free gift. On the packaging and some of the pages we displayed the text "FREE GIFT," and the parcel was sent from the USA to Germany. The customs declaration read: "Contents: Gift." There was not a single German on our marketing team—and we soon learned our mistake.

In German *das gift* translates literally to "poison," "toxin," or "venom." Free or not, most Germans were not willing to sign a customs form to receive their *gift*. And you can't really blame them.

Now perhaps this example seems more about securing good translations, but the greater point is that the more you can make your advertising make sense and appeal to the local market, the stronger the message will become. It's about being in on the *inside* joke, speaking to people the way they speak to each other and using images that comfort rather than offend.

We call this concept "transcreation." It's the process of simultaneously translating *and* localizing a message while maintaining style, tone, and content.

Remarketing and Retargeting

These are two similar concepts that impact how much an advertiser can afford to pay you for your efforts. If you understand that an advertiser will work toward an acceptable margin, then you will also understand that the stronger the marketing effort on the backend, the more money they will have to pay you for your work. Conversely, an inability to monetize what they have means they will be impoverished when you ask for fair compensation. In short, you don't get paid unless they get paid.

Remarketing is the advertiser's efforts to turn the customer's lifetime value into that projection. It is, very simply, following up on a purchase. Remarketing is typically done by email, SMS, and targeted audiences. Check any offer you want to run to see how the advertiser tries to sell you more products.

Retargeting is a similar concept but done through digital media for those who visited your webpages. Ever wonder why viewing a travel site means you are soon-after bombarded with advertising related to vacations? *This is retargeting.*

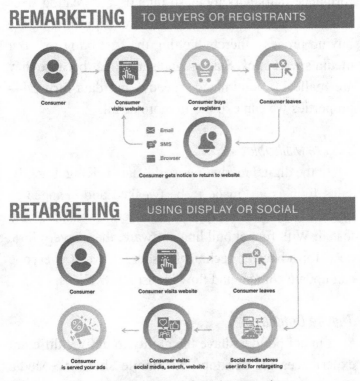

Figure 6. Remarketing and retargeting.

Building the Funnel

By now, you have figured out that media buying is hard work, new platforms emerge, regulations change, and tastes shift. In order to earn attention (and hopefully an advertisement click!), you need to constantly innovate and find new ways forward.

The last thing Media Buyers want is to earn a click only to watch their customers fall off because of a sloppy funnel with sub-optimal content. This is why performance marketers focus so intently on creating sales funnels. Funnels have a unique way of optimizing the buying process, thereby getting the best *bang* for your media spend *buck*. Sales funnels are great because they are malleable, optimized, speedy, and data-forward—properties we can explore in more detail.

They're Malleable

In the digital marketing world, data is King. Luckily, sales funnels are made to be tweaked and changed as needed. They can be rapidly adjusted, duplicated, and tested. With funnel building software, there's very little need for advanced technical resources. Most everyone can update content and flow in just a few clicks.

They're Optimized

Funnel builders have the ability to deliver different experiences for desktop and mobile shoppers. Media Buyers must understand *how* their customers are buying; failing to deliver an optimized experience will negatively affect customer acquisition costs and significantly threaten profitability.

They're Speedy

Page load speed is paramount for bringing scale to products and services. Some studies show that each additional second of load time equates to an 8% drop in overall conversion. Funnels can solve this problem. They have elegant, minimalistic code, and many automatically compress media assets such as images, videos, and fonts.

They're Data-Forward

Funnels are designed for performance marketers. These are people who make marketing decisions *based on data*—on what they see, rather than on what they feel. That's why almost every funnel-builder has a built-in analytics dashboard attached to it. All key performance indicators are front-and-center. They're easily understood and updated in real-time. This allows marketers to track performance, assess profitability, optimize, and scale.

If funnels were a campfire, their reporting dashboards would tell you when to dump water on the embers or when to add more wood to make it roar. Funnels make the best s'mores.

Designing and Updating the Funnel

If there is already an identical or near-identical funnel, you will want to secure that and see if there is paid traffic. Always be on the lookout for competitive funnels.

Various ways to find funnels include:
- Keyword searches and clicking on paid advertisements
- Targeted social media
- Free and paid spy tools

In the fast-paced and ever-evolving world of online marketing, it is absolutely necessary to monitor new market entries and new advertising strategies. As media platforms update their advertising policies and ad approval processes, they require you to know the standards you must adhere to where you're marketing. Note: Major platforms apply different rules to different parts of the world.

You can invest in tools to help you find competitor advertising or just employ some old-fashioned internet research and elbow grease to gather exactly what you need. Many tools pull ads and overlay data, which can be useful in determining how far and wide the ad is running. In general, if an ad is running week after week, and you've started counting it in months, it's only running because it is profitable for the advertiser.

Tools will tell you about audience demographics and engagement levels, media spend, page visits and traffic trends, product and ad lifecycles, and many other crucial points. Or you can research for yourself using keywords in search engines, or by adjusting your demographic characteristics in social media so you can receive the ads for your target audience.

Most Media Buyers will have several different search and social media accounts for the purpose of receiving relevant, current ads.

When you are ready to build your funnel, you will want to make use of one or more of the funnel building tools. They all use similar templates, and let you easily build your content into them.

Some of the main funnel building tools are:

- Clickfunnels
- Unbounce
- LeadPages
- Convertri
- CTRwow

All of these products are good. Clickfunnels is by and large the most popular in the affiliate community and the Clickfunnels teams offer great support and motivation to many young affiliates. They have a lot of users for good reason; however, if the product is hosted by Clickfunnels the experience tends to be slow, so a lot of people use the tool to build and then migrate the content to a faster hosting service.

Unbounce is a great product for lead generation and was built for that purpose. LeadPages is much like Unbounce and has many users for lead generation. Convertri is quick and easy, and many of my Media Buyers use it because of this.

CTRwow is our DFO product, built exclusively for e-commerce. CTRwow has two benefits over the others: It has our high performing e-commerce templates, and it is built to be fast. It also allows for quick and easy A/B testing.

Putting the Funnel into Practice

We love media buying at DFO Global, but ultimately, it's the sum of our parts that makes us valuable in the e-commerce space. In particular, Ron Robinson, founder of BeautyStat, can attest to that. Ron spent most of his adult life in beauty product development. A cosmetic chemist by trade, he created some of the most well-known beauty brands for companies such as Estée Lauder, Lancôme, Revlon, and Avon. If you're a female, you've probably used at least one or many more of his products in your life.

DFO Global and Ron got together as he was taking a break from working at the large cosmetic companies. He was keeping his well-read blog, *BeautyStat*, updated with product reviews, but was mostly interested in our young influencer business. We hired him to oversee it because he was charismatic and understood the nature of that business, given his background.

Long story short, the influencer business was not destined to be one of our core competencies. It was shuttered after two years, but it pushed us— and Ron— to new heights.

As the influencer business was winding down, we challenged Ron to think about a more entrepreneurial path. Beauty was his passion, why not create a brand? His ingenuity as a chemist and our marketing and e-commerce capabilities made a good match. In a short period of time, *BeautyStat* evolved from a blog to a standalone beauty brand with breakthrough skincare technology. The BeautyStat brand, as we know it today, was born.

In its first year and a half, BeautyStat did more than five million in revenue. Its success can be broken down in several different ways:

- **Good PR**. Ron has appeared on Good Morning America, QVC, Oprah Magazine, and more. He continues to take advantage of good public relations opportunities, which have caught the attention of retailers. Almost all beauty retailers in the USA and England now carry BeautyStat products.

- **Influence**. Ron's time with DFO Global as head of the influencer business allowed BeautyStat to bring on both micro influencers and global celebrities. This has pushed BeautyStat's messaging to—and garnered sales from—an even wider group of customers.

- **Industry Knowledge**. Ron understands the need for exclusivity (in the form of partnerships and patents), the need to be different, and the need to be on par in terms of product quality and presentation. BeautyStat's flagship product is a vitamin C product, which is known for being unstable. Ron and his team found a way to stabilize it and then they patented it. The result is effective, doesn't require refrigeration, and notably gives users a tingling sensation on the skin when used.

- **E-commerce Chops**. Ron's experience as part of DFO Global has yielded rewards. Our performance marketing capabilities realigned his perspective on how to sell a product online and outside of the USA.

At DFO Global, we've helped the BeautyStat team build out webpages that specialize in sending users down sales funnels and through to purchase. Our back-end technology powers most of their online marketing, which makes load times fast and conversions easy.

We continue to act for the brand in an agency capacity, facilitating its media buys on Facebook, Google, and other platforms. BeautyStat uses us as a fulfillment and customer service provider.

Making it Happen

One of the best things you can do to understand funnels is find some good ones with live traffic and follow them to see how they work. You can click and find out for yourself how a customer gets moved through from an initial headline to a purchase at checkout. BeautyStat Cosmetics, for example, offers some great funnel examples that will help you learn to build your own. I recommend you check them out.

Once your funnel is working and you're bringing in customers and sales, there's only one question left, which I bet has been on your mind for a while now: "How do I get paid?"

CONCLUSION:

CAN YOU EARN
A MILLION DOLLARS?

Finally, the question you've been waiting to ask. Go ahead, ask me: *How do Media Buyers get paid?*

Media Buyers are employed by various kinds of companies and they buy various types of media, so it's probably not surprising to learn they can be compensated in various ways.

That said, although there are many types of Media Buyers, there are some typical ways to get paid. Remuneration is linked to the three main categories of employment for a Media Buyer. These are categories of *agency*, *corporate*, and *performance* media buying—and each remunerates a little differently.

Agency

This is likely where the majority of Media Buyers will start. They will be employed by a digital agency and tasked by that agency to build or work on advertising campaigns. They will purchase digital media for those campaigns.

Agency work is almost always judged on Return On Advertising Spend (ROAS). ROAS is a marketing metric that judges the campaign by comparing dollars in revenue generated to each dollar spent on advertising. If your ROAS is 3:1, this means you are making $3 in consumer revenue for every $1 you spend on ads. ROAS allows agencies to quickly and effectively communicate to their clients the value of their advertising efforts.

Here is a sample ROAS calculation: Your agency spends $30,000 with Facebook during the month. The campaign tracks $120,000 in sales revenue to the client. Therefore, the ROAS is a ratio of 120,000 to 30,000 or 4:1. The agency can go to the client and say that for every dollar on advertising spent they can expect $4 in consumer revenue.

Agencies will typically charge their clients a stand-by fee per month to cover the creative development, and then a percentage of ad spend between 8–20%, perhaps with some additional performance bonuses for hitting certain metrics.

Media Buyers in agencies that are working for clients on ROAS are typically paid a very generous salary and a bonus or performance metric based on the buys and total spends they achieve. The earning potential is very high because clients—especially during certain periods of the year—will buy as much media as is available.

Corporate

Many companies employ Media Buyers for a variety of activities related to their business, including:

- Generating sales leads
- Generating direct consumer sales
- Promoting with paid media on social media

These Media Buyers are often on budgets with metrics of achieving so many leads, registrations, or likes for a certain cost. They are usually remunerated with a base salary and perhaps a bonus for meeting their quotas.

Performance Media Buyer

Well, I promised at the start of the book that you could earn a great deal of money buying online media. Upwards of a million dollars a year, to be precise: if you work hard and savvy. Time for me to make good on that promise by explaining where and how.

Performance Media Buyers get paid the most because they take on the most risk; they can be paid nothing, or in fact lose money, but they can also bring in more than a million dollars a year. The Media Buyers who work for my company who are not part of our agency are entirely performance paid and *this is why their earning potential is huge.*

Let's take a look at the example above, for the agency model, where we generate $120,000 in sales, which is represented by an average cost to consumer of $100, or 1,200 sales (1,200 sales with a $30,000 spend is a cost of acquisition of $25 per sale).

Now imagine that you go to that client and say that instead of paying the agency $30,000 a month, *let me buy your media for you.*

Likely the client will say they are happy with their agency and their 4:1 ROAS, why would they want you to buy your media?

So, you pitch the potential client:
- You will charge only $25 for every customer
- You will deliver as many customers as they request
- They can keep the agency and you will provide customers *over and above* the agency buy

This scenario creates an interesting situation. The agency is paid cost, plus charges $30,000 for the media, and probably makes $3,000 on its spend.

You, however, the performance buyer, need to deliver customers and get paid $25 per sale. You are highly motivated to optimize the ad, improve the ad, improve the placement, target more specifically, understand the product, and build performance. If you can produce a client for $15 in advertising spend you make $10 per customer acquisition.

This means that compared to the agency, which spends $30,000 to make $3,000 and generate 1,200 customers, you make $12,000 for generating the same number of customers!

You make four times more than the agency, in this example, using the same media spend. However, you also took on the risk for yourself. If you failed to reduce the per customer media spend you would perhaps have lost money because your costs over $25 per acquisition are not covered.

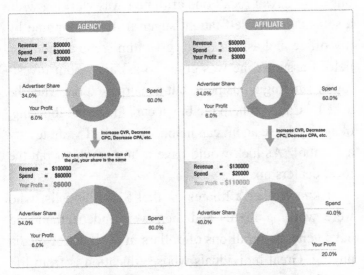

Figure 7. Agency versus affiliate media buying.

Thus, the rewards are huge if you succeed. And that is why we're here.

I asked the DFO Global Performance Commerce CFO how many Media Buyers are both working for us currently and working with us as affiliates, then I asked him how many Media Buyers we've paid over a million dollars. His answer is impressive. As of the writing of this book, in the relatively short time since founding our online division of DFO in 2016, we have paid more than one hundred Media Buyers more than $1 million, and fifteen Media Buyers more than $10 million. We are just one company amongst many in performance marketing. *Who are these people earning this incredible profit?*

Performance Media Buyers are literally men and women from all walks of life and all education levels. In our early days I recall one affiliate I was working with, a self-made and self-taught super affiliate, stopping by my office and asking me to give him some advice and help. I assumed he was going to ask me about investing or running a business, but he surprised me when he asked, "Can you help me buy a car?" I started thinking, okay, my lease agent can help... He said, "I want to buy a Lambo!" As luck would have it, my neighbor ran the local dealership.

I know other affiliates on that $1 million list who were working for us and then went independent and have generated millions of dollars in revenue for media buying. Great individuals whose education is from life experience, hard work, and meeting and talking to people. Getting to know how people think and operate. We also have affiliates who have gone the other way; they started as an independent affiliate then moved to work exclusively with us and have earned the million-dollar check totals.

Like I said at the start, you could be the next person to do this.

Our Coffee Date Comes to an End

I have told you all you need to know about what it takes to be a Media Buyer. You have asked the tough questions and learned about the Prime, headlines, angles, using images, writing great copy, targeting, tracking, media available for purchase, and funnel building. These are the Media Buyer's tools, and they can all be learned best by working with someone who is a master.

Maybe you have the right combination of personality and skills to be the next great Media Buyer. *If you do, I want to work with you.*

This business is growing every year. It is one of the last great frontiers for making big money online. In 2020 alone, global e-commerce sales rose by just under four billion dollars with an estimated growth rate of 8.2% per year through 2024, according to Statista.

There is enormous potential for those bold enough to work hard and make the most of this amazing opportunity.

But this job isn't just lucrative—although that is certainly a big part of it. It's an incredible challenge where you are constantly presented with moments that require innovation, quick thinking, and creativity. You will never, ever be bored as a Media Buyer.

As a Media Buyer, you will take the lead and create on your own, or at times you will direct a variety of professionals from artists to writers to programmers to sales teams. You will in short order become an expert on the online space. You will take on risk and reap reward.

As a skilled negotiator, you will use your networks to get the best possible deal to maximize profit for yourself and your clients. You will gain an acute understanding of what makes people act and what factors motivate them. In short, you will be part Don Draper, part Gordon Gecko, and part Sherlock Holmes (without the depression, alcoholism, jail time, and cocaine!).

When I look back, I am so glad I followed my gut and stuck to my interests and got myself into this exciting business. Could I have made a good living as a trial lawyer? Sure, a great one—I was doing that. Would it have been interesting and rewarding work? Probably. But there is just no way I would have gained the range of experiences I've had, that I could have worked with the great people I've worked with and made the vast amount of money I've made—if I hadn't got into e-commerce.

I don't regret my career decision for a second.

Are you intrigued? Is your head buzzing with ideas and are you excited by the thought of becoming a Media Buyer?

We need good people: smart, driven, *with great instincts*. And when they succeed, we succeed. That's why I wrote this book. I have just given you a distillation of knowledge acquired over many years of hard work because for us to continue to grow and maximize the huge growth that this industry is experiencing, I need intelligent, thoughtful, talented, hungry, goal-oriented Media Buyers.

If you're still reading, then I am willing to bet you think I might be talking about you. So, let's get in touch. Email me at bcran@dfo.global or go to the DFO Global website to apply for one of the Media Buyer jobs posted there. You can also take our Media Buyer aptitude test, and whether you work for my firm or another I want the world to know about this amazing opportunity. I'm waiting to hear from you, and so are the HR departments of major advertising agencies and affiliate companies. Perhaps you'll go big, hang up your own shingle, and buy media as an affiliate. I'm waiting to pay you a million dollars or more.

GLOSSARY

A list of terms used in this book and in media buying.

A/B testing (split testing) means dividing your traffic to two different pages in order to assess the pages on a selected metric (average order value, click-through rate, etc.).

Abandonment rate is the percentage of people that leave an e-commerce store without paying for what is put in their cart.

Above the Fold or Hero Section is the immediately visible webpage content on a user's screen. It excludes any content users must scroll to view.

Acquirer (Acquirer and Acquiring Bank) is a financial institution that authorizes you or your company to use credit card processing like Visa, MasterCard, Amex, and Discover cards.

Ad copywriting is writing specifically for an advertisement.

Address Verification Service (AVS) generically refers to any service that verifies a consumer's address.

In credit card processing, acquirers use AVS to establish whether the address provided on a transaction is the same address on the billing statement of the consumer.

Adsense or Google Adsense is an advertising platform run by Google, enabling website owners to display text, videos, and images for advertising.

Advertiser is the owner of a product or service being marketed.

Adware is usually a toolbar or browser extension that allows advertisers or networks to serve ads to a consumer.

Affiliate Link is the HTML or JS code that tracks the customer/visitor on the merchant's website and any conversion for which the affiliate would receive a commission.

Affiliate Marketing is the business of promoting advertisers' products or services in exchange for commissions.

Affiliate Network is a type of agency that focuses on bringing affiliate traffic to an advertiser's offers.

Affiliate, Associate, Publisher or Pub is a person or company that drives traffic to advertisers' offers for a commission.

Algorithm is a concept or string of ideas stated in rules to be followed that form the basis for programmers to build software.

Analytics or Online Analytics is a technology or team that helps track and analyze the performance of a website or online marketing campaign.

Application Programming Interface (API) is a communication protocol that lets one computer system talk to another computer system and exchange information, even though each might be built in completely different programming languages.

Arbitrage in performance marketing is the practice of buying and reselling web traffic, hopefully for a profit.

Attribution is a credit given to one or more affiliates based on rules established in the affiliate program for commission eligibility and prioritization. The rules can impact how much an affiliate makes. For example, the *first touch rule* means the affiliate that first delivered the customer receives the commission, even if a second affiliate delivered the customer to the checkout page.

Authorization is the process of granting permission to someone to allow them to give orders or make decisions to take action. Advertisers usually need to grant authorization for specific affiliates to run traffic to their offers.

Average Order Value or Average Cart Value (AOV or AOC) is the average total amount charged to the consumer upon settlement.

B2B (Business to Business) refers to an exchange of product and services between two businesses. For example, selling paper from a wholesaler to a retail store.

B2C (Business to Consumer) refers to the exchange of business or transaction conducted directly between a company and consumers. For example, selling paper from a store to a consumer.

Backend or Backend Development refers to the development and software, processes and system, which tracks credit card processing, fulfillment, and customer service for the advertiser.

Banking refers to the various credit card processing methods on the backend of an offer.

Banner Ad is an electronic ad in the form of an image often called a banner that is available in many sizes and displays on a webpage.

Baseline in analytics is the starting metrics before testing.

Bid, in an auction for traffic with providers such as Google or Facebook, is the maximum amount of money that an advertiser is willing to pay each time a consumer clicks on an ad.

Bounce Rate is expressed in percentage and refers to the percentage of visitors who navigate away from the website or funnel.

Brand Bids or Brand Bidding or Brand Name Bidding is the process with search engines to buy a brand name as a key word and/or the policies that must be followed.

Browser is a software application that enables a user to display and interact with text, images, videos, and other information typically located on the web.

Browser Fingerprint is when a consumer's computer visits a website and engages in a digital handshake.

This allows the consumer's computer to pass along to the website information such as IP address, time stamp, browser and browser version, monitor resolution and dimensions, plugs-ins and many more things that can be used to identify the computer if it visits again.

Bundling refers to the marketing strategy where several same or similar products or services are combined together and sold as one package, usually at a discount.

Buyers Persona is a demographic or psychographic representation of your prospective customers based on data or speculation.

Cache generically is temp memory storage and in marketing is an area of storage space on a computer that temporarily stores web pages that a user has visited through their web browser. Items that are cached load faster.

Call To Action (CTA) is a request to the consumer to do the desired action that the webpage provides, or which pushes the consumer to act.

Cap is when the network or advertiser restricts how many sales can be made. CAP is used to control sales levels for risk management or inventory controls.

Chargeback is a credit card transaction that is reversed by the consumer or the card issuer on the basis of a complaint relating to the charge. This is a forced return of money to the consumer, in contrast to a refund.

Click Bot is a program generally used to artificially click on paid search listings or ads in order to inflate clicks to generate more PPC revenue.

Clickthrough Rate (CTR) is the percentage of people that clicked on a button or moved down a sales page. Every step in a funnel has its own CTR.

Cloaking is the use of technology to hide the actual advertising from a traffic platform or select group. Uber, for example, is known to give police and enforcement a different advertisement for its vehicles than what consumers receive.

Co-branding is a website or page, to which affiliates send visitors, which includes their own logo and branding.

Cohort Analysis is a type of behavioral analysis that breaks groups into subsets of related groups.

Comma Separated Values (CSV) is a file format that easily allows users to exchange data knowing fields are separated by a comma.

Commission Rate is the rate of income an affiliate receives for generation each sale, lead or click-through to a merchant's website. Performance is often cost per sale or CPA.

Content Marketing is the promotion of products/services via a website with content about one or more subjects related to the product or service.

Conversion is a successful acquisition. Tracking software tracks conversions.

Conversion Rate (CVR) is the amount of people expressed in percentage that committed the action of the CPA.

Conversion Rate is the percentage of visitors that land on your website who complete a sale.

Conversion Rate Optimization (CRO) is the process of enhancing the user experience of a website to improve the chances of convincing the visitors to complete the end goal of a sale transaction.

Convert (Conversion) is a visitor who takes a desired action such as a sale or registration.

Cookies are bits of code in the consumer's browser used to report metrics and activities of the consumer, including buying activity.

Copyright is the right granted by law to the author or originator of certain advertising, graphic images, or videos that protect the advertising developed for a product from being copied.

Cost Per Acquisition (CPA) is how much we pay for the acquisition of one customer. With CPA one price is paid irrespective of how much they buy or their lifetime value. Sometimes the action is not acquisition, but a registration or other event.

Cost Per Click (CPC) is when the advertiser pays a publisher/affiliate when the ad is clicked on.

Cost Per Install (CPI) is reserved for downloading content from the app or play store.

Cost Per Lead (CPL) occurs when the advertiser pays for a visitor's information submitted in the forms of email, phone number, address, and so forth.

Cost Per Thousand or Cost per Mille (CPM) is the cost per thousand of impressions.

Coupon or Coupon Code is a popular form of on-line sales promotion, usually in the form of a code entered into a promotional box during checkout to trigger a discount or special offer.

Creative is a banner ad or text link used by an affiliate to promote a product. Also used as assets for a webpage.

Cross Channel Marketing (Omni Channel Marketing) is selling, tracking, and monitoring the actions/movements/data of visitors and customers across all devices and channels.

Cross Promotion is a way to attract more customers by joining forces with another brand after the same target market.

Crowdsourcing is a sourcing or funding model that lets people vote with or without their money to assess a project, product, or service as viable.

Custom Acquisition Cost is the cost associated with acquiring a new customer via the web or any other medium.

Customer Acquisition Cost (CAC) is a metric that refers to the cost associated with acquiring and convincing potential customers.

Customer Lifetime Value (CLV) is a metric that predicts the total value that would equivalate the lifetime relationship between any given customer.

Customer Relationship Management (CRM) refers to a system that integrates front and backend systems to organize and document customer contacts, purchases, customer service, and technical support.

Dashboard is referred to as a hub for important business and performance data that enables a snapshot overview of a particular matter.

Data Feed, Web Feed or News Feed is the process to update webpages with real time information.

Dead Link is a hyperlink that does not lead to the content it once did.

Deep Linking is a hyperlink that indexes with search engines that allows consumers to find content that might be otherwise buried.

Demand Side Platforms (DSP) are user interfaces for Media Buyers that let them buy advertising in real time.

Demographics is a term that refers to specific information about a population or a target market.

Destination URL is a specific location within a site where the user who clicked on the ad should be directed.

Direct Offer is where the advertiser gives the offer to an affiliate without a network. It may or may not be exclusive to the affiliate.

Discount Code is a promotional discount that consists of unique letters or numbers that compute and activate a discount or special offer.

Discount Rate is the amount charged to a merchant by the acquirer for processing the merchant's daily credit card transactions.

Display URL is a URL shown to visitors on paid search engines and appears below the ad text, often the same URL as the site's homepage.

Distribution Network is a network of websites or search engines with their partner sites on which paid ads can be distributed.

Domain Name is controlled by the worldwide organization ICANN where domain names are obtained for a fee on a first come basis to identify a unique website.

Double Opt-in is a process in which a webpage collects information to have it confirmed by the consumer by emailing, texting, or calling.

Dropshipping is a business practice whereby instead of buying and holding inventory, a company uses a third-party provider to supply and ship the products the business sells.

Duplicated Clicks refer to clicks that have been considered to be duplicate based on a unique session identifier and duration's set in the tracking and controls of the webpage.

Dynamic Content is information on webpages that changes based on database queries or is changed automatically based on user factors such as geography, language, operating system, and web browser.

Earnings Per Click (EPC) refers to the average amount of money you earn each time someone clicks one of your affiliate links.

Email List is a list of email addresses and other personal information about subscribers.

Email Marketing is promotion of products or services via electronic mail.

Engagement Rate is a metric used to measure how much a visitor gets engaged to the given piece of content or ad.

Events is a way to track the activities of a consumer on a website or in a funnel either before or after a conversion. For example, Google Tag Manager (GTM) can be used to monitor specific activities or events as the consumer clicks on a call to action, passes on certain content, moves to the checkout fields, or buys an upsell.

Exclusive Offer is where a network or affiliate has the sole rights to drive traffic to an offer.

First Party Cookie is a cookie that is readable by the website as a user is visiting.

Frequently Asked Questions (FAQ) is a document that answers the most common questions on a particular subject, product, or service.

Front End or Front End Development refers to either all that displays to the user, or software development of what displays to a user.

Fulfillment is a sequence of steps a company undertakes to process an order from factory or warehouse to delivery to the consumer.

Funnel or Funnel Sales is the process of curating a product or service and selling it through a pre-set flow designed to keep the consumer engaged and within the funnel until purchase and certainly without the distractions of an e-commerce storefront.

Geo is the country where the offer is valid or can be run.

Geographical Segmentation is the ability to determine from which geographical area web traffic is coming.

Geotargeting is a method of targeting audiences geographically.

Google Analytics refers to a free web analytic service provided by Google that allows a website to be linked for the purpose of tracking web traffic and provides statistics that are useful for SEO and marketing purposes.

Gross Sales is a metric for the total sales of a company, unadjusted for the costs related to generating those sales.

Guaranteed Earnings Per Click (GEPC) is provided by the network or advertisers to the affiliate to assure them a minimum earning per click.

Hypertext Markup Language (HTML) is a computer language that is used to position and mark webpages to bring them live online and is also used for email templates.

Hypertext refers to text on a computer that will lead the user to other related information via a link.

Impression is an advertising metric that indicates how many times an advertising banner, link, or product on the page is loaded and potentially viewed.

In Bound Link is a link on a third-party website that points to your website, also known as Backlink in SEO talk.

In-house refers to the fact that the Agency or network owns the offer or services.

Incentivized Traffic or Incent Traffic occurs when the consumer is rewarded for participating or registering. This kind of traffic is considered lower quality because the person is compensated for their click.

Influencer is a person or group that holds the ability to influence the behavior or opinions of others via social media.

Infographics refers to graphical visual representations of information, data, or knowledge intended to present data easily and in understandable format.

Insertion Order (IO) is an advertising term that refers to the advertiser's consent and agreement under the agency's terms to run advertising. It is also a general term for a contract to run traffic which is made between a network and an advertiser or affiliate. Such contracts contain terms of best practices and protect all parties.

Interchange is the process of authorization and settlement of credit card transactions.

Internet Protocol Address or IP Address is a unique key assigned to individual electronic devices or networks.

Interstitial is a concept of loading between two ads, or between an ad and a checkout, with a further ad that often has the purpose of solidifying the qualities of the product or service being sold.

Invalid Clicks are clicks that fail to register to the destination URL.

Inventory refers to the advertiser's stock of goods.

Issuer or Issuing Bank is a financial institution that issues credit cards such as Visa and MasterCard, Amex, and Discover cards.

JavaScript (JS) is a high-level core front end language that helps drive the world wide web.

Key Performance Indicator (KPI) is the predetermined metric to meet in order to determine whether or not the marketing is successful.

Keyword Domain Name is the use of keywords as part of the URL to a website to position an advantage with some search engines.

Keyword is a word or phrase entered into a search engine's search field.

Keyword Phrase refers to two or more keywords combined to form a search query.

Keyword Tags is a META tag used to help define the primary keywords of a webpage.

Landing Page or Splash Page or Webpage are used interchangeably and refer to the first page of a funnel or website where potential customers land.

Lead is someone who has expressed an interest in the product or service, usually by registering with an email or phone number.

Lifetime Value is the aggregate amount the consumer will pay to a company once they become a customer.

Listing is information that appears on a search engine's results page in response to a search.

Logistics is the management of goods and services or resources between the point of origin and the point of consumption to meet the requirements of customers or corporations.

Lookalike Audiences arise when the traffic provider is supplied with data on a group of people, and that traffic provider then offers up traffic of the same or similar characteristics. The data can be offered in the form of email, phone number, or tag clicks.

Malware is software that is often secretly installed on a consumer's device, or perhaps deceitfully installed, that can monitor the consumer or feed the consumer advertisements.

Media Buyer is a person that buys traffic from providers such as Google, Facebook, TikTok, Outbrain, Taboola, or other platforms.

Merchant Account is an account with a payment processor for settlement of credit card transactions.

Merchant is another name for advertiser or retailer.

Minimum Bid is the least amount an advertiser can bid for a keyword or phrase and still be in the auction.

Mobile Marketing is a promotion of products or services via a smart mobile device.

Native Advertising refers to a type of advertising where online content is created for paid promotion of a brand but resembles the publication's editorial content.

Niche Site is a website oriented toward a very specific topic or audience.

Non-Incentivized Traffic or Non-Incent is the opposite of incentivized traffic; no reward is offered for participation beyond a nominal item such as a newsletter.

Offer is a product or service that is being offered to a visitor by an advertiser.

Opt-In is a consumer that has subscribed to an email newsletter, electronic service, or online agreement.

Opt-In List is a list of email addresses of customers who have agreed to be contacted by email.

Optimization is changes made to improve webpages, specifically their position on search lists or page conversion metrics.

Organic Search Results are non-paid search engine results. These are webpages that search engines determine to be the most relevant matches for the search keywords.

Outbound Link is a link on a webpage leading to other webpages on other websites or domains.

Page Rank is an indicator of the value of a webpage that is used for ranking in search engine results and is governed by a proprietary formula by search engines.

Page Speed or Page Load Speed is a measure of how long it takes to load the key content on a webpage.

Page View is a term for the loading or screen presentation for a single webpage.

Paid Placement is an advertising program where listings are guaranteed to appear with high rankings in response to a particular search term or particular page.

Paid Search is referred to as a pay per click strategy used by a large number of affiliates to drive users to their own site or directly to a merchant's site.

Pay In is what the advertisers pay to receive a conversion.

Pay Per Click is a program where an affiliate receives a commission for each click they refer to a merchant's website.

Pay Per Impression is an advertising pricing model in which advertisers pay based on how many users were served to their ads.

Pay Per Lead is a program where affiliates receive a commission for each lead that they generate for a merchant's website such as completing surveys, contests, sweepstakes entries.

Payment Threshold is a minimum accumulated commission an affiliate must earn to trigger payment from an affiliate program.

Payout is what an affiliate gets paid for a conversion.

Performance Marketing is a type of marketing where one business rewards one or more affiliates (or pubs) for a set action (normally a sale) by a user referred due to the one or more promotional efforts made by the affiliate.

Performance Pricing Model is when an advertiser pays based on the set agreed upon performance criteria, such as a percentage of online revenue or delivery of new sales leads.

PIN or PIN Submit is a type of lead generation offer where simple personal information is collected and sent as a lead.

Pixel (Tracking Pixels) is the primary tracking method that uses scripts in URLs passing between websites to track actions or conversions.

Postback or Postback Pixel is a tracking concept where the CRM of the advertiser advises the traffic source directly of any conversion or registration confirmation.

Presale Page or Advertorial is a kind of splash landing webpage that contains content resembling a newspaper article or review of the product being advertised.

Query is a word or phrase a searcher enters in the search box.

Referral Program is a program wherein the network, agency, or merchant pays a commission to the party that refers business.

Refund is the company that charged a consumer credit card reversing the charge.

Remarketing is the process of selling to your existing clients.

Retargeting is a process of selling to visitors to your web properties.

Return On Advertising Spend (ROAS) is a metric that measures the amount of revenue your business earns for each dollar it spends on advertising.

Return On Investment (ROI) is a performance measure used to evaluate the efficiency of an investment or to compare the efficiency of a number of different investments.

Return Visits is the average number of times a user returns to a site over a specific time period.

Run or Run an Offer refers to an affiliate driving traffic to an advertiser's offer.

Software as a Service (SaaS) is a method of software delivery and licensing in which software is accessed online with a service subscription, rather than bought and installed on individual computers.

Search Engine Marketing (SEM) means using paid search media to buy traffic

Search Engine Optimization (SEO) is the process of maximizing visitors to a webpage through integrating content or keywords that prompt search engines, such as Google and Bing, to rank the page higher on the list results in a consumer's search.

Secure Server or Secure Socket Layer (SSL) Server is a web server for data encryption, mandatory for sites accepting credit cards because it protects consumer data.

Shopping Cart Abandonment is when a user leaves a shopping cart with an item or items in it without completing the sale transaction.

Shopping Cart is a software application or concept that retains the items the consumer selects to buy either at the end of the session or on a later date.

Single Opt-in is simply the registration by a consumer of their information. Single opt-in is less valuable than double opt-in because it does not have confirmation after data registration.

Smartlinks allow a webpage to customize and personalize the configuration of the product or service based on what is set as a trigger on the link.

Spyware generally refers to software that is secretly installed on a user's computer and that monitors use of the computer in some way without the user's express knowledge or consent.

Targeted Marketing is the process of identifying specific groups for the products or services being sold.

Third Party Cookie is a cookie created and readable by a website other than the website a user is visiting.

Third Party Offers are offers that are not owned by the network that is seeking affiliate traffic.

Tracking is a method of monitoring and retaining information on referred sales, leads, or clicks.

Trademark (^{TM}) is a proprietary term that is usually registered by the merchant with the Patent and Trademark office to assure its exclusive rights to use but can also be a common law mark established by use. The superscript (^{TM}) means the mark is filed or in use, and the "R" in circle (®) means it has been accepted for registration.

Upselling refers to a sales technique that persuades a customer to buy something additional to their initial purchase.

User Experience (UX) is an overall experience using a particular product, system, or service, especially expressed in terms of how easy or pleasing it is to use.

User Interface (UI) is the way in which everything is designed to facilitate users to interact with an application or website.

Vertical is a category of consumer products or services, for example: health, beauty, electronics, and so forth.

Visit is a measurement of activity attributed to a single browser for a single session.

Visitor Segmentation is a differentiation of users to site by categories such as age, sex, language, geo location, and so forth.

Web Analytics refers to a set of strategic methodologies that study the impact of a website on its users, mostly used to access and improve the effectiveness of a website.

ABOUT THE AUTHOR

Bruce P. Cran is the CEO and Co-Founder of DFO Global Performance Commerce, a multinational company with over four hundred employees and in excess of a billion dollars in sales. He went from being the youngest lawyer to argue before the Supreme Court of Canada to heading one of the largest performance marketing companies in the world. An expert in identifying and capitalizing on e-commerce opportunities in emerging markets and new media, Bruce possesses an acute understanding of the dynamic and ever-changing sphere of international business. Earn a Million Plus is his first book.

ENDNOTES

1   Ogilvy, David. 1983. *Ogilvy on advertising*. New York: Crown.

2   Vonnegut, Kurt. 1999. *Bagombo snuff box*. New York: G.P. Putnam's Sons.

3   Shelley, Mary Wollstonecraft. 1992. *Frankenstein*. New York: Everyman's Library.

4   "Frances Gerety," De Beers Group, accessed February 18, 2021. https://www.forevermark.com/en/now-forever/a-diamond-is-forever/frances-gerety/

5   Pichère, Pierre, and Cadiat, Anne-Christine. 2015. *Maslow's hierarchy of needs*. Namur, Belgium: Lemaitre.

6   Ogilvy, David. 1983. *Ogilvy on advertising*. New York: Crown.

7   Popeil, Ron. "Ronco Food Dehydrator and Veg-O-Matic FULL Infomercial," YouTube, accessed February 16, 2021. https://www.youtube.com/watch?v=IFugZm6TWzk

8   Hick, W. E. 1952. "On the rate of gain of information." *Quarterly Journal of Experimental Psychology* 4(1): 11-26.

9   Bly, Robert W. 2013. *The copywriter's handbook: a step-by-step guide to writing copy that sells*. New York: Henry Holt

and Company.

10   Glaser, Milton. "Using Design to Make Ideas New," filmed 1998. TED Video, 14:39, https://www.ted.com/talks/milton_glaser_using_design_to_make_ideas_new/transcript?language=en#t-281023

11   Ogilvy, David. 1983. *Ogilvy on advertising*. New York: Crown.

12   Ogilvy, David. 1983. Ogilvy on advertising. New York: Crown.

13   Bly, Robert W. 2013. *The copywriter's handbook: a step-by-step guide to writing copy that sells.* "The 4 U's Formula for Writing Effective Headlines." New York: Henry Holt and Company.

A free ebook edition is available with the purchase of this book.

To claim your free ebook edition:

1. Visit MorganJamesBOGO.com
2. Sign your name CLEARLY in the space
3. Complete the form and submit a photo of the entire copyright page
4. You or your friend can download the ebook to your preferred device

A **FREE** ebook edition is available for you or a friend with the purchase of this print book.

CLEARLY SIGN YOUR NAME ABOVE

Instructions to claim your free ebook edition:
1. Visit MorganJamesBOGO.com
2. Sign your name CLEARLY in the space above
3. Complete the form and submit a photo of this entire page
4. You or your friend can download the ebook to your preferred device

Print & Digital Together Forever.

Snap a photo

Free ebook

Read anywhere